## Advance Praise for *The Wolf...*

Carolyn Lewis populates her pages
from Michigan's past, among them lu...
Americans and Beaver Island's Mormc
and speak relevantly to readers today. ...istence of fierce
family love amid severe strife, extraordinary hardship alongside
radiant joy and the duality of northern Michigan as both beautiful
and brutal emerge as the themes of this posthumously-published
collection. Elements of tragedy, fable, folktale and romance
surface by turns, sometimes in the same story, and Lewis'
writing is particularly rich in imagery. *The Wolfkeeper* merits
a place on the shelf of all who appreciate Midwestern, rural
storytelling, or simply darned good writing.

—CARI NOGA, author of *The Orphan Daughter*

More than a decade ago, I had the pleasure of reading a few of
Carolyn Lewis' short fiction. Having all of her stories collected in
*The Wolfkeeper* is a special gift. Each tale reflects her attention
to detail and craft, her themes are timeless and true. Carolyn
worked slowly—each story is an elaborately constructed
tapestry—weaving place, character, and time. From the opening
sentence to the final period, the reader is pulled into another
world. These are stories to remember, to savor, to read again.

—AARON STANDER, author of the Ray Elkins series

In this posthumous collection, readers will discover beautifully
wrought tales populated by wolves, wild children, unruly
Mormons, mystical elders, majestic horses, flutes of sacred bone.
Carolyn Lewis fearlessly explored the intersection between
regional history and timeless spirit, between plainspoken
humanity and family myth, between the lore of First Nations and
the bittersweet lives fashioned from the inadequate materials
of human love and loss. In these clear-eyed and otherworldly
stories she offers haunting characters and
a narrative grace readers will not soon forget.

—ANN MARIE OOMEN, author of *Pulling Down the Barn*

Illustrations by Tajín Robles

Readers are encouraged to go to www.MissionPointPress.com to contact the author or to find information on how to buy this book in bulk at a discounted rate.

Published by Mission Point Press
2554 Chandler Rd.
Traverse City, MI 49696
(231) 421-9513
www.MissionPointPress.com

ISBN: 978-1-950659-12-8
Library of Congress Control Number available upon request
Printed in the United States of America

"Dancing, Feather Light" was first published as the lead story in the *South Dakota Review* (1993), edited by Geraldine Sanford.

"The Religion of Loss" was fist published in the *Sycamore Review* (1999) and described as "a unique new voice" in the Novel and Short Story Market.

"Wings to Follow" was first published in the *Nightshade Nightstand Reader* (1995), an anthology of rural writing, with a foreword by Fred Chappell, poet laureate of North Carolina.

"How the Mormon Wives Stole the Gold from Daniel Ben Long, King of the Mormons" was a semi-finalist in both the Pirate Alley William Faulkner Award and the Heeking Group Foundation Award and was first published in the *North Atlantic Review* (2001).

"Defiant" was first published in *Kalliope* (1997), edited by Maxine Kumin, poet laureat of New Hampshire, who nominated the story for the Pushcart Prize.

# THE WOLFKEEPER

*stories by*

## CAROLYN J. LEWIS

MISSION POINT PRESS

# CONTENTS

*In the land there is a longing*
*and the longing is in the people,*
*and the people who come to it*
*have a name for it they never speak.*

# FOREWORD

My wife Carolyn Johnson Lewis died much too young and before she could find a permanent home for the stories contained in this collection, most of which had been published in various journals. Such publication, while rewarding and noteworthy at the time, is ephemeral. Once the next issue of the particular journal appears with its new roster of writers and their works, that which was contained in the previous number begins the long slide into obscurity where only the most diligent searcher, with a fair amount of luck, can find it.

Carol's work deserves a far better fate. When I take off my husband's hat and put on that of a practicing writer myself, I long ago recognized the special quality of her work. Not that I was in danger of forgetting or downplaying that recognition, but I was reminded of it one evening when the dementia that would take Carol away from me had robbed her of so much, but when she retained the ability to process the spoken language, I was reading to her, as I sometimes did.

I had chosen "Wings to Follow," one of her own stories, easily available as we had a copy of the journal in which it had appeared lying on a table nearby. I wanted to see how she would respond to hearing her own work. That she recognized, and responded to, her own words pleased both of us. But I was not ready for my own reaction when I finished reading the story, one I did not remember well although it is likely I had read it at some stage of its composition.

When I came to its end, I looked over at Carol. "You nailed it," I said. "You absolutely nailed it." I was expressing my admiration for the craft so obviously and beautifully executed to bring that story to a satisfying conclusion. Doing so, in my view, is the peak of the storyteller's art, craft in the service of formidable talent.

Her disease prevented her from offering to the world more such wonderful reading experiences. This collection, at least, preserves and makes available between the cover of one volume, the stories that demonstrate ever so forcefully how great a loss her premature death is to the reading world.

—*Stephen Lewis*
*Old Mission, Michigan*
*June 2019*

# THE WOLFKEEPER

# THE WOLFKEEPER

Through the opening mouth of dusk, a cabin appeared, the glow from a wood fire flickering in its window.

A wolf curled her paw around the rough rim of the door. Nudged it open with her black nose. Stood. Looking in.

Arms dangling, mouth open, wisps of hair rising from his head, an old man sat with his head thrown back, a blanket slipping down his knees. A small fire danced on the hearth. From a hook, a vine basket swayed, five loaves of bread warming. The dirt floor picked up a glow from the fire.

She turned, lifted her muzzle, sniffed. A human scent emanated from the road, one not known to her. She pricked her ears. Up the cliff three young pups yapped and sputtered, their distant cries floating down.

"Is that you, old friend?" His voice rose drowsy from sleep. "One, today for them?" He sat forward, "or two? Come, come. Don't hesitate. What keeps you?"

She swung her head back to him. Whined. The white of her fur lay soft as moonlight rising in through the window.

"Here, I won't hold you. I can hear your young

ones fussing all the way down here. Come. Take." Fingers white from gripping the arms of his chair to steady himself, he rose and, shuffling to the hearth, slipped his hand into the vine basket above, cranked his arm like a baseball pitcher winding up and, holding onto the back of the chair with his right, let fly with his left.

He heard her jaws creak open, tension in the air as the bread arced up, the slight scraping sounds her front paws made as they left the floor, a slight *harrumph,* and an intake of air. With a crunch of teeth on bread, she thumped down with a slight whump on the dirt floor. A kind of chortle issued from the back of her throat. A blow of air. He imagined a slight bow by the sounds, which he heard, but could not see. A slightly bent front leg, a paw tapping, and then ... ah ... there. She walked a few paces forward and lowered her chin to his knee. One pat, two. He stroked her ears with his fingers, smoothed the fur down over the hard bone at the top of her head. The little knot behind her right cheek he rubbed softly, and her throat where the hair grew soft and the skin was somewhat loose. He sighed.

"Yes," he whispered, softly. "Some day you'll bring your children to see me." These things he heard: the brush of her tail on the half-open door. The slight intake of air as she paused looking back, how the wind, whistling in, changed tones as she trotted out. He had once seen her habits, her movements, how she crouched before she leapt for the bread. But now he just heard her front legs come up, the *harrumph,* of her catch, the shift of bread into her mouth, the snap of her jaws. Her quick trot to the front door, the stop to look back, the slight padding sounds her paws made on the earth outside and then just the wind: a long howl and moan through the yellow standing grass. When it whistled into the cabin, he walked forward and leaned on the door. It creaked lightly on its leather hinges, for winter had not yet invited spring in.

Clenching the loaf in her teeth, she trotted across the meadow and, winding among the boulders, began her ascent up cliffs of blue stone. Pines of enormous height hid her, trees so old their bark resembled the cracked clay of a dried riverbed. Even the wind went around those trees, their needles too dense to maneuver through.

◆

Beneath a late winter moon that painted the meadow blue, she stood. Touched the rough door with her forefinger.

The logs had been halved, then hammered down with bark placed vertically over them and pounded on with a flat stone. Wooden pegs had been shaped by a knife, carved of hard oak, not scrub, which the builder would have had to leave the area to find. These things she knew, also.

The leather straps on the door swung in. She stepped in beside them. The aroma of freshly baked bread filled the air. Another smell, too. Something wild and rank she couldn't quite place. Old-man smell, maybe?

The dirt floor showed the marks of a broom. A vine basket over the hearth held four bread loaves, warming. There was a crude sense of domesticity here: the table wiped with a hand, the saw and hatchet marks on the chairs, the very smell of dust caused her to put her hand to her nose and stop a sneeze. Just like a man, the Ojibwa girl thought, and turning, found him asleep inside a big log that had been cut to fit through the door, dragged indoors and hollowed out. Inside it, softly snoring, the old man slept.

Lifting one of the two chairs from the table and setting it

next to his bed, she sat gazing at him sleeping, then out the glass window, for the clouds drifted in the sky like a man dreaming.

Who's to say what old men dream? Do they speak to the rabbits they stumbled across as children in the field, saying thank you, you can go now, it's okay? Do they fall deep into the eyes of God that pass through the night as stars? Do they leap from their dreams just before morning, thinking they are still boys with a wagon on a hill? Or do they wake in the day, wondering, somewhere, somehow, if they have always been old men?

A finger twitched.

From his lips, a whisper. Dark shadows crossed the bridge of his nose. Could they be because his face lay in the light of the moon that shone through the window: a cloud, and then another, passing over?

He could be two or three hundred years old living as he does, she thought.

Twitching his fingers, he coughed. And when his eyelids lifted, there was only white where blue used to grace his irises.

"So. You have come to visit?"

"Yes."

He lifted his head as though he heard something.

"There is no one else here," she said.

"There is but you are too young to recognize him, Mitena. You do not know Death's musty smell." He coughed, with a rasp, and from under his blanket brought a handkerchief to his nose.

Glancing out the window, she took in the pine trees on the other side of the meadow. They looked so inviting, those limbs so wild in the wind. She sighed, and with her finger, she wiped at a tear that ran by her nose.

When she turned toward him again, his eyes had closed.

She shook his shoulder.

"I'm still here, unfortunately." The wind came tapping on the door then. With gentle fingers, it nudged that door open. "But it is time for you to leave."

Silence entered the cabin.

The wind blew the door wide, swept around the old man and the young woman, and pranced out along the meadow path, where it sat, waiting.

◆

The wolf stood on a boulder among jack pines, watching the ripples in the harbor the boat set in motion below. Turning, she trotted the few yards to her cave, where she curled around her pups, who were pushing the loaf of bread around with their noses and batting it with their paws. Each time a cub batted it, another cub took a bite.

The next evening, at the appointed time, she trotted down the cliff path, around the boulders and through the spruce forest, until she stood once more before the cabin door. A little nudge, a solid push, and she padded softly in. Sniffed the air. Nosed the man's bedding. Scuffed beneath the table for crumbs. Standing beside the fireplace where only one ember was aglow, she sniffed, pawed the dirt floor. Lay down beside his bed. Smelled the day old aroma of bread.

And stood.

She might have stopped there, turned and gone out and checked in again later, but she didn't. She could have gone to get her pups, brought them back to lick the crumbs from the floor, but, she didn't do that either. She didn't, in fact, do anything for a long while, but look over her shoulder from time to time. Eye the door. Whine a little.

Scuff the floor with one paw.

Lie down.

Stand up.

Then.

Padding to the door, she turned one last time to look back. And, tail quivering, leaped. Opened her teeth and brought the vine basket down. Bread in mouth, she trotted out, tail banging the door wide behind until the wind rustled in and those leather hinges bounced the door off the back wall and slammed it shut.

◆

Pulling the blanket up to his nose, he slept deeply, fully, his clothes and coat and even his hat still on. The late afternoon light shifted into dusk, dusk into dark, and dark into lightening morning.

For two days he stayed wrapped in his blanket, even the lowering afternoon light too much to abide by. And he wondered whether he should still go on. Doesn't age allow one to stand still? Rest from one's endeavors? Hadn't the archangel seen he was ready to go? His chest rose and fell, the breaths slight, the air a mild whisper, until the light coming in the window seemed too much to abide by. Why was Gabriel not beating his wings against the window? Why did God keep an old priest here?

A nagging thought came into his mind: an aha! There are those details one must perform before death will come. A letter not finished. A thought still unwound. The prayers of penitence? Which sat him straight up in his bed.

Swinging his feet to the floor and standing, a little wobbly, he moved to the hearth and lifting his arm up, felt for the vine basket overhead. Felt again. Huh. What? In its bottom was a gaping hole. Bending down, scuffling across the dirt floor with his palms: crumbs! How many loaves taken? His hand found one more.

When the moon had passed twice over the window, the wolf did not come, nor in the third morning did she come. He began to surmise that hunters had shot themselves a white pelt that would bring a pretty penny. He mourned the loss of her company, the soft ears, her silky nose, falling finally, into a dark slumber from which he did not wake to eat. Or sweep the floor. Light the stove. Or make the bread. Weak, he was unable to rise and bank the fire. He became instead, part of the long winter's sleep on the land, the one that comes back to the north in April, the one that's never really gone. A sleep deep and troubled. Feverish. One that doesn't think spring will come. He coughed, too, with a wracking deep in his lungs.

The wind opened the door and howled in, snuffing the fire's last red embers out, but he hadn't strength to rise and close it. And he wondered: had God finally opened the door and sent for him? He imagined the great feathered wings of Gabriel, his trumpet calling, some masterful way in which God would say:

Come. Rise.

Yes, Lord. I'm ready, he whispered.

But, when he opened his eyes, there was only light sifting across the room: dusk to dark, dark into light. And then: dusk, dark, lightening, light.

He languished. Three days, four? Half an hour, an hour?

And then.

He felt the air turn one way, not another. The way vibration circles around a room when there are two in it, not one. How the feeling shifts to include what has stepped inside. And he knew, suddenly, that she was sitting at the open door. The odor of wet fur drifted to him, and he knew it was raining by the scent her fur brought in.

She scuffed the floor.

Stood.

Lowered her head.

He heard the small creak of her neck. A little murmur in her throat, heard her crawl along the dirt floor, felt her place her jaw on the top of his knee. Leaning up on one elbow, slowly, stroking the top of her head with two fingers, he sat up, then from beneath his blanket pulled out the remaining loaf. He sank his teeth in. Tore one chunk off. Chewed. Felt it go down. Immediately, strength entered back into his body. He knew this was the way of the dying. One can subsist one's final days on only a cherry, a bit of bread, a drink of water.

He called her to come, stroked the lowered head. Pulling off a rough slice of the bread he offered it. She rose, then seemed to kneel, for her head and front paws went down, which he heard through the tiny bones in her elbows creaking. Her paws scraped the floor. Grasping the loaf gently from his hand, she let his fingers brush her head. Once. Twice. She lowered her head, lifted it, placed her chin on his knee where he sat now, the bread in her mouth silly, like a child who has crammed its mouth full. He felt her breath on his hand. Stroked her soft ears.

She turned, looked back at him once, which he heard by the hesitation of her paws on the floor, the turning creak the little bones in her neck made, her breath a little shorter.

And she went out.

◆

Snow fell again, in soft petals that melted so so quickly, they left nothing more than a slight whitening on the dried husk of winter's ground.

Scraping the door open, Mitena nudged him in his log

bed, but he did not move. She noted the coldness of his skin, his hands fixed together in prayer. And when she turned and began to move the door to close it, she saw the maze of tracks that led from the sill to his bed, some so old they seemed from another century, and those which hadn't even yet the skim of dust on them. The tracks of a large animal that walked like a dog.

She looked from the floor to the door to the bed. And in the end, she swung the door wide and nudging a stone against it so it couldn't close, left. Knowing the animal had come every day, for the print of its body was there in the place where no dust lay: the imprint of its legs, its head and belly, the long tail, dust shadows on the floor where it lay sometimes one way, sometimes the other.

◆

Several days later, she returned to his cabin. Brushing out the last of the leaves that swept in, tucking five fresh loaves of bread she'd brought with her into the vine basket, she hung the basket up and closed the cabin door. But as she started across the meadow, there were whisperings in her mind. Stepping back, swinging the door wide, she went in and when she came back out she didn't close that door, but left it open just enough so that someone *could* come in, and pay homage.

From the cliff, the wolf looked down, and then it raised its voice, for it longed for something it could not name. Below, Mitena began to sing the songs of her forefathers, the songs of her mothers, and between the two of them, the wolf up cliffs of blue stone and Mitena on the meadow path, their voices rose together, howling.

# DANCING,

# FEATHER LIGHT

O-ko mes-se-maw, her Ojibwa name, lets her bed clothes drop from her too-thin shoulders. Her hands rest on top of the other in her lap. They are so transparent the bones rise like mountains through her skin.

She is me-de-mo-gay, tiny and brown and wrinkly, an old, old woman.

She is sad this morning. I touch her, stroke her fine white hair, smile at her. I lift the wooden flute to play, but she brings my hands down again. She shakes her head.

"Aiee," she says simply. "I am dying, Granddaughter."

"Oh, o O-ko." I mock fight with her, the flute in my lap, my hands gently slapping hers, but she grabs my arm, pointing west, through her bedroom door, across the old kitchen with its worn linoleum and scratched wooden counter, through the three-paned, rollout rusted window shut tightly against the winter. Outside, parallel to the frozen bay, the snowy two-lane state road of M-22 runs north

*13*

through Omena, Michigan, a town of rusted pickup trucks and hunters' taverns about a mile up, then south the other way, weaves around the tourist center in Suttons Bay and on down, the ice of Lake Michigan crumbling the road's edges like petrified toast all the way.

In between, our tribal lands are the only thing we have.

"Mau-tchi au-naw-quot, the bad cloud, used to always come from there, across the bay from Ningobianong, the West. Now, mau-tchi- au-naw-quot comes from the four directions, takes my screen door off its hinges, and pours water into my house. You see? It's not just me. The wind itself is confused.

"Yesterday, before you came back, when it rained and snowed at the same time and the wind came in from the West, I took the rugs off the floor and put the cat and the blankets on the kitchen counter. Then I went upstairs into the rafters and waited to be washed out of the bay and into the great lake. Kaw-win ke-taw-gawsh-ke-to-se tchi-gaw-ke-so-taw-wod mau-ni-to."

The last thing she said was the only thing my mother ever said in Ojibwa: You cannot hide from God. She said it to my father at a time when it was the one thing he didn't know.

I was here yesterday. I am here every day now. There was no rain and no snow together, or wind from the west or wind from the east either.

I don't know when she will begin to lose me. Will it be piece by piece — today I am a girl with a too sensitive face, unnotably dark hair and large eyes set too close together, tomorrow my dead father, my sister, brother, the next day myself again — or will it be all at once she will look up from her soup bowl with those ancient eyes, and suddenly and forever see me as a hostile stranger?

O-ko mes-se-maw sighs and looks at the ceiling. "I'm so cold," she says, "I'm very cold."

I take the hot water bottle and fill it from the pot on the

---

stove. Then I get into bed with her, nudge the bottle against her and put my arms around her. She is such skin and bones.

"Sometimes death is not a bad thing," she whispers into my shoulder.

"No," I say. "No, sometimes it's not." I speak the words with the tenderness I feel and rest my cheek on the top of her head. I rub her arms to warm her up. She is very cold.

She lays her head back on the pillow, closes her eyes and speaks softly of many things I do not know.

Sometimes she is like that, telling me a story until her voice slows and softens. It is then, when the sentences turn into mere murmurs, that I fear the worst. I bend lower and lower, down to her mouth to hear the very last word, afraid one lost sound will mean that Death has arrived, so quietly I could not know in advance.

While she lives, it's not as if there's any danger of losing the thread. She wakes up talking and goes on talking exactly where she left off, as if she had only stopped for a moment to remember how to describe the sun on her husband's hair in the morning, or a wisp of a name coming back, long forgotten, or as if she simply stopped to stretch, like the cat on the hot stove, when in truth, time has quietly vanished.

My fear, more often than not these days, knots up tight with strong rope that cuts off air so quickly I must remember the rhythm: breathe in, breathe out.

I edge my shoulder out from under her sleeping head, reach for the broom behind the door, and give a few strokes beneath the bed today. I wander out into the kitchen to stoke the fire and make hot soup for her. It's not like there's any place else to go.

The back room off the kitchen, where we keep wood for the iron stove, is damp. Cold drafts from the lake winds sweeping across the ice blow in through the cracks in the walls and the holes in the plastic that cover the windows.

The kitchen and the bedroom in the front, which is all there are to the house, if you don't count the rafters, is toasty from the huge and black Franklin wood stove.

It is testimony to my grandmother that she won that stove in a poker game with a cherry farmer across the bay. She won a lot of things during her time there: a good shovel, a lug of sweet cherries, a silver watch with hands and no face that kept good time for thirty-seven years.

They thought she cheated, pushed the jack of diamonds up her dress or down her sleeve before the game, but they couldn't prove it. She was scrupulously honest about matters of their children whom she cared for, so they shook on the deal, assuming, perhaps, she was honest about cards.

Even so, it took twenty-two Ojibwa dressed in choke berry juice, including seven children under the age of nine, three grandmothers, six old men, five pregnant mothers, one man with a broken leg, and one dog with a very crude owl that the children painted on his back, which is all there was in camp at the time, to convince the cherry farmer that the stove was a done deal, won fair and square with an inside straight. The cherry farmers, she said, were a little stubborn about their possessions, but in the end they were usually good on their word.

I take a few pieces of kindling and two big logs from the wood pile that my brother keeps cut and stacked next to the big loom in the back room, glance out the back window, then stagger back to the kitchen. It would be easier to make two trips, but one burdensome one seems more appropriate somehow, fills me with heavy accomplishment that two light trips could not.

A few steps from our back door, the ice spreads its skirts out five miles or so across the bay toward the great lake where the wind sweeps in ferociously. If you stand there, facing straight off to the northeast, that's the direction of Papa's fishing hole. The ice is smooth here, below our three stone steps, rougher out in the middle where the wind is strong.

Hands palm-down on the cold burners, I stand staring out the kitchen window, mesmerized by the snow drifting along the ice. Postcards for the tourists are deceiving. The beauty in the snow hides the breath of the ice bear, the scent of the hunter.

Out there, Papa's fishing hole has frozen over with him under it.

"He walked into it," the tribal police said. O-ko mes-se-maw cried for her son. For a little while, I felt relief.

I still try to imagine that misstep into the freezing water in the face of a blinding white snow storm, but all that ever comes to mind is a picture of a dead deer, and the deer is not him.

I don't think Grandmother ever understood what happened out there. I don't think I do either, but I don't really care. Papa wasn't so good to my sister and my brother and me. Or to my mother.

I try to understand O-ko mes-se-maw. He was her son, the only child she had left. Her other boys, all three older than Papa, had died, one under a jack-knifed semi-truck on an icy road, the second in a hunting accident, although I don't know how, for he was only the cook and never left camp to hunt. The other one, well, a bear clawed him up.

So I couldn't tell O-ko what Papa did to us; she looked so sad. I think she knew, though. There was just something in the way she looked at me sometimes, before he died, held me close and rocked me — and I am no young child. Or perhaps she thinks I am him, her baby again, his world so small it included only her.

But I am her child, since Papa died. That's what she calls me; and she no longer rocks me. It is me who now rocks her.

"Child!" she cries out. "Child, come over here and play your flute for me." Sometimes I play. In fact, the more miserable I feel, the better the song. But I'm not always compliant. And she's not always good-natured.

I remember when the tribal police handed her Papa's fishing pole, a limp grey minnow still swung on the hook. They didn't even have the decency to unhook the thing and throw it away before she saw it.

O-ko took it off herself, gave them one of her disgusted looks, and walked out the back door and down to the second stone . From there she threw that minnow as far as she could onto the ice, which wasn't very far, stooped down, washed her hands in the snow, shaded her eyes from the glare on the ice, then walked back, pulling her shawl close around her. She went back to work on the loom without having said a single word.

They shrugged and then left, and I went with them. From the car, I watched a seagull swoop for the minnow, pick it up and swallow it, flying. I don't know how those seagulls survive out there in such bitter cold. I thought they were here only in the summer.

I had to sign some papers up at Administration. One of the tribal police, the short stout one, suggested I take the nasty job of sorting through Papa's stuff, and what could I do? Say no? Besides, I was morbidly curious to see what the old place looked like, although the memories are so bad I had bugs crawling under my skin, walking up to the door. I dragged my boots through the snow the whole way.

I hadn't been in the trailer for years. What a mess, junk everywhere, unwashed clothes, beer bottles, shirts and undershirts yellow, grey, torn or worn or just wadded up and thrown in apple crates on the floor. Even the screens in the windows were ripped out, the stink of fish everywhere like an old bear's den. I can't believe we all once lived here.

There was not a single sign of my mother, dead these many years. I am sure I grimaced, but in my heart I was glad she didn't live to see this.

I didn't tell the police either, what he was like. What for, my brother said when he stepped in past the police guard to look around the trailer. Let it rest, he said, and showed me where his arm had never mended right, broken in three places from a fight he'd had with Papa years ago during that long cold winter that Mama was so sick.

"Over what?"

"Over nothing, what else?"

I saw how thin he was, vacant, like he was hollow, nothing showing through to the outside, but I was wrong, like I've been about him before, never guessing what was in his head. He had something stirring in there all right. "I'll be back," he touched my arm, no hug I could have really needed, and whisked out.

"To do what?" I lifted my hands to the empty trailer. I threw the junk in a garbage bag one of the policemen gave me, tucked a few food cans from the cupboard into my coat pockets, and went out to talk to them.

"What do you want to do with it?" they asked, looking everywhere but at me. Oh, they knew all right, what he was like. That look said everything. They were embarrassed, I could tell. But for who? Him or me?

"You could torch it," I said, suggestively.

"Against the rules," they said, firmly.

"So what?"

"Rules are rules."

"It's a hazard ... All sorts of bacteria in there. Dangerous, maybe, to let something like that stay out here."

"It's a place for someone to live. We've got plenty of people who need it. So why don't you clean it, and we'll get a family in there next week. Okay?"

A few days afterward, I put on my gloves and hat and old worn and torn Navy coat, my prize possession because the buttons are pure brass, and got a second ride up to Administration to answer some questions. Two of the tribal police took me out into the woods, and showed me where the trailer used to be.

I couldn't help myself, honestly. I tried to look grim, the grieving daughter, but, hell, what good was it? I smiled when I saw the charred ground and the seared tree stumps that surrounded the spot. I touched the greasy earth, sniffed the fresh singed air where the trailer had stood, and knew what my brother had done.

I didn't accept the ride back with them, but scampered through the woods toward O-ko mes-se-maw and home, watching the gulls rise from the lake all the way.

There was nothing more the tribal police asked from me. They knew something about my father anyway, enough I guess, from the days he spent inside their jailhouse, head leaning back against the cold plywood wall, eyes closed, arms crossed on his chest like he was frozen there.

Windigo, we called him, peering in from the crack in the side window behind the police desk. "Nyah, nyah! Can't catch us, old ice bear!" But I was very young then and not easily frightened yet. How much changed in so short a time.

That day — that day got stranger. While I was gone, O-ko mes-se-maw walked down the beach, climbed up the twisted tree and fell out of it onto her head. It was night time before we found her, and by then the tribal police were becoming my friends. I guess they thought I'd lost a lot that day.

I don't know what she was doing up there.

"He's up here," she cried from her perch as we came

racing down the beach. "Up, up, up!" and she was laughing. I didn't know what to make of her, sitting high up on a branch of that demented tree, but then she fell, like in slow motion. We ran, helter-skelter, from spot to spot, but we missed her entirely. There's so little to her, she didn't even crack, she made no sound, just wisped this way and that, then touched down, softly, like a few feathers drifting and settling from the breeze. So I just took her hand, brushed the tribal police off, and we walked home, a blanket around her thin shoulders. There I tucked her into bed and she fell right to sleep.

Maybe she had seen Death up there and went to meet him. Maybe she thinks the tree is her friend. Maybe she was looking for my father. I don't know. I can no longer guess, and Death is so very close.

I am so afraid, Grandmother, I can't tell you. Aren't I supposed to be taking care of *you*?

She is talking herself awake. I've been standing here daydreaming again; I guess I'm a little tired now. These nights and days ... Well, it's not my place to complain. And yet ... I do, if only silently.

I feed her hot chicken soup with a spoon. She smacks her lips after every spoonful with her toothless gums coming together and apart again like a silly *au-mick,* a beaver without teeth, to make me laugh.

She finishes some of the soup, thrusts it back into my hands with good strength and takes up the little loom, clacking it back and forth, back and forth, clack-clack, clack-clack, a constant, almost humming sound when worked with her expert hands. The head of a snowy owl forms swiftly beneath her fingers. She hums as she works, a melancholy song I do not know.

I set the bowl down on the floor beside the rocker, draw a blanket over her legs, and push: forward, backward, gently, creaking, nodding as the light in the house changes from white to yellow, to reddish-yellow, dims a little, gathers up its edges, and folds itself quietly into black.

I startle awake, seeing only the branches of trees gesturing through black windows.

Now. Now he is here, so close I can smell the breath of the ice bear, the reek of fish, that one red light signifying ...

No. No, it is only the paling red of the peep hole in the stove's fire box.

A sudden sharp crack shakes the walls. I clap my hands to my ears, remember O-ko mes-se-maw and snake my arm over to find her. We wait silently, I, flinching under a blanket in the rocking chair, she under the covers in her bed, our two hands joined mid-air in between. "Is it him?" But she is usually calm, then, in the dead of night, having asked, as if the final moment brings the strength to see Death open the door and walk in whole. She drifts off, but the second crack comes in without warning. It is deafening; the house trembles.

It is the ice, all across the bay, breaking apart with a "boom!" that sends me leaping to her side, where she gathers into me like a frightened fawn. Then it slams together again, forming open seams with the force of mountains rising straight up out of the sea.

The earth first rose up under the ice, O-ko mes-se-maw says.

I don't know. I wasn't there.

Not now, but in the mornings when she sleeps the longest, I slip outside and walk across the ice to find the narrowed seams, newly opened, their frozen sides forced mere inches apart. Inside the seams, ice walls, twisted and jagged, descend one or two feet to the bay. I stand, one foot straddling either side of the crack, frost crackling against the skin on my face. Down there, the grey-blue waters gurgle and suck at the ice.

Holding my balance as long as I can, toes just touching either edge, I close my eyes and imagine the seams pulling apart beneath me. The ice moves slowly, with magnificent strength, each edge slipping away from the other, until ... I fall down in between. The seams crash together; the water so blue and silver and cool, death so sudden it takes your breath away.

Then I turn, leap the crack and race to the house, sliding into the steps — once I sprained my ankle doing this — up to the door, open, slam, throw off my boots, leap into bed and under the covers, huddling into Grandmother who cackles a little, and pulls the blanket close around me.

These days I skip the huddling/comforting part. I race to the back door, but wander in quietly to the rocking chair then, and sit, knees drawn up.

"Brooding," she says. "You're in your brooding mood again. Go sit with the chickens."

I yawn now, stretch my arms above my head, hands clasped, and crack the bones up and down my neck.

She is awake now. She has lit a candle beside the bed and is working on the loom by candlelight. She must have slept when I did.

The ice is quiet.

I can see O-ko's breath in the air.

The damn stove needs more wood. It is my master; I have become its slave. I leave the rocker, bow low to the ground before the Franklin's awesome, fat-bellied presence. O-ko chuckles.

As I grope in the dark for a particularly big piece of wood in the back room, the "boom!" strikes, sharp and close this time. I stop, listen, startled. If there is no tree, what brushes against this side of the house, scrapes the shingles on the roof? Surely he's there, just outside the window, waiting for her.

I race back, shove the stove full of any scraps of wood I can find fast and light the oil lanterns. We have never had the quick safety of a light switch.

Now what? Tend to detail. Oh, yes, supper. Stew will make a good supper. I stand, waiting for it to bubble, counting bowls and spoons as if I could multiply two by one hundred and fill my time counting them. How many ways can you count to two?

"Aaiiee," she cried out yesterday, sick with the fever. "Death is coming, as sure as the bottom-most scales on Grandfather Snake rattle silently across the snow. He leaves no trail and no visible path. He should not be here in the winter, Granddaughter!" She gets positively visionary sometimes.

Stir, stir, stir, but it doesn't bubble. An old Ojibwa saying: Never watch the pot, or you will find that it will be waiting for you.

There are times when O-ko deals well with Death. For one thing, she named the black cat after Papa, gave it a place to sleep and feeds it well, so she'll always know where Death is: a thin black cat asleep and smoking on a hot stove. But this is a joke, and we both know it is not a very good one now.

We eat the stew in silence, only the soup and spoons make noise.

"Here," she hands me the loom when we are done eating. "Here is the West," O-ko smiles at me and runs a transparent finger along my cheek to bring my thoughts back to her. I nod to show I am with her.

"West is the black circle. There lie rainbows, thunder, death, autumn."

"Here," and she points to a red circle. "Here is East, the

place of birth and hope and herbs, the place of Spring." She nudges my ribs with her bony elbow.

"This," she says, now in Ojibwa, a thin finger on a yellow circle, "is the South, from where the summer warmth comes." She is so full of spirit when she's like this, and so ... *here*. Was I supposed to get a message back there about the East?

"And this," she traces a white circle, "is the North, brought by the white goose and the snowy owl who scares the children back to their houses at night. Here, you do the body of the owl." I weave it in, working more carefully than she to get it right. I stab my finger five times with the needle.

I have to weave the design in by hand without the loom. She is trying to teach me the old way. I am a very unwilling and difficult student. I find the old way extremely tedious. I am not an Ojibwa child of much patience or virtue. Or is it just that some things bore me to no end?

O-ko catnaps again. She snores, very loudly for a thin old woman. After a while she nudges my ribs with a knobby elbow. "Are you awake? I have to tell you something."

"So tell me." I settle more comfortably on my right side facing her, and lean my head onto my propped-up hand. The loom rests quiet between us.

"See the tree down there on the lake shore, all gnarled and twisted with the seasons? Whipped by the wind that tree is. What do you think of it?"

"It's interesting-looking." I don't want to say it looks half-dead because I know where *that* will go. We've had enough conversations on Death today. "It's unique; and, it's almost pretty." It is also the tree that she fell out of. It's also pitch-black out there. Should I tell her I can't see a thing of what she sees? But then, what else is new? I'll just go along.

She sits up and looks in my face with disbelief. "Pretty? Pretty! Hmph. *You* are pretty. *That* is the Tree That Lives

Forever. Some call it the Twisted Tree." And she is quiet for a moment, humming "hm, hm, hm" to herself.

"I'm not pretty, Grandmother."

She lifts my chin with her fingers, strokes my face, then agrees. "True. You have a chipmunk's face." She grins, snaps her fingers against my cheek, then kisses me on the ear.

"Granddaughter, once that tree grew straight and tall; now it folds in on itself." She pauses, gets up, looks toward the back door that leads to the ice, listening for a few seconds, then sits back down on the bed where I am, her hands in her lap.

"I am that tree, Granddaughter. That tree is my memory, bending against things it wants to forget, circling and embracing the ones it loved. Your father, ... well." She seems content to leave it there, leans her head back against the wall, lifts her knees so the bedclothes rumple around her, places a hand on each quilt-covered knee, and bounces up and down like she is bouncing a toddler on her stomach, and smiles.

I always have this image in my head:

I see in my mind that one second before the deer, still alive from the bullet, looks into the hunter's eyes and judges itself. It thinks, or would if it could, should I have jumped to the left instead of to the right, as if that jump, with the hunter so close, would have made a difference, life instead of death. As its vision clears in death, it sees the hunter raise a knife over its heart and is terrified, not that it will die, but that it will die mistaken. Was I mistaken about something? About Papa? And my mother ... I don't think so.

But this is my vision, not my grandmother's. This is the difference: in O-ko mes-se-maw's eyes, the deer does not criticize its own movement when it is the one who stands just out from the trees, seeking the hunter in the midday sun.

She has made my father the ice bear, the sought-out hunter, and her lost baby, all in one. She cries out for him to come, is frightened when he seems near, yet rocks her arms like he is the baby in them, while I lie panicking, dreading every creak in this old house, each one his wet boot step.

"It's the seasons," she speaks gently. "I've fought all my life to stop them from coming. Yet I couldn't stop time when I was happy to see tomorrow, to think things could be better than today. When the children were little, I loved life and fought against its forward movement, all at the same time. Now," and she turns to look at me, her eyes covered with a film, "you must not be sad."

I shake my head, trace the stitch patterns on the quilt, sit numbly beside her. Breathe in, breathe out. That's all there is. Breathe in, breathe out. See how easy it is? But I don't seem to be able to loosen the ropes that cinch my chest.

"Look west, look east, then north, and south. All that you see, you'll see again. The people of this country, they hunted us in snow when the ground is barren and shot us in the summer heat when the ground is fertile. What is different, Child?"

"Only the ground." I feel resigned.

"Only the ground. Now," O-ko pats my hands and looks into my face cheerfully. "I'll tell you a story."

I don't feel particularly cheerful. I want to run like hell so I won't cry. My chest hurts and I feel the bed falling away from me with O-ko on it. She's smiling, and there's just me, stranded in space, one frightening second before I fall. What's down there, Papa? Is it you?

She plumps up the pillow behind her, orders me into the kitchen to get raspberry tea, and then leans back like a proper society woman with her pinky out and sips it. I have to smile, finally, at her antics.

I don't know what time of night it is.

"First, the moral. The wind is a thing to watch and be careful of. No-din, the wind, can lead you, and it can kill you.

It is best, in both cases, to listen to what it has to say, even if you have to cover your ears to hear it." I laugh, out of control, and skootch in beside her, nudging up close to keep us both warm.

"There was an Ojibwa man, living some ways off tribal lands, who wished his grandchildren, living some ways away onto tribal lands, would come to see him. Of course, they had no way to get there.

"One spring evening he was sitting outside the back of his house, having a peaceful smoke, watching the eastern sky for the first stars. While the smoke from his pipe drifted lazily up to the sky, No-din, the wind, took the porch off the front of his house, flung it over his head, and set it down in the branches of a tree right in front of him. The man looked at it for a while, shrugged, then nodded and said it would make a good tree house for his grandchildren. So he went around the garage, got a hammer and nailed the porch to the tree. But the grandchildren didn't come.

"In the summer, No-din came back and tore the boards loose from the tree and flung them into the next field, in the general direction of our tribal lands. So the man gathered his tools and hammered the boards into a playhouse for his grandchildren. It must be, he said, that my grandchildren don't like to play in trees; they prefer fields. That is why they don't come. Then he dismantled his own house and rebuilt it in the field so as to be closer to their playhouse. But the grandchildren still didn't come.

"In the fall, No-din lifted the entire playhouse up and set it down without disturbing a single board, on top of a hill overlooking the tribal lands where the grandchildren lived. Ah, the man said, my grandchildren like to play in the long grass on the hills. So he took apart his own house and rebuilt it on the hill next to their playhouse to be near them. But the grandchildren didn't come.

"Then it was winter, and four seasons had passed and the man felt such despair at not seeing his grandchildren that he thought he would just give up. That winter there were no bad storms and No-din never came in force. Spring came. The man took apart his house and the playhouse and went down onto the tribal lands to tell his grandchildren that they could use the wood for whatever they wanted. 'It was going to be a playhouse for you,' he said, 'but, well, it doesn't matter.'

"'A playhouse!' they shouted. 'A playhouse! Grandpa's making us a playhouse. Mama! Daddy! Come see, come see.' And so the man rebuilt his house for the last time right next to where the grandchildren lived and put their playhouse in between the two houses. And you know what? The grandchildren came and played every day.

"There are many bad stories about the wind, Child. That's the only good wind story I know. The wind's power and knowledge are immense. Na-bwa-jaw-tchig ... They that are wise, are also careful.

"And since I am wise," O-ko beams at me while I clap my hands in delight at her story, "I make sure that I am close by my grandchildren."

I pull her head toward me and kiss her cheek. She pushes me off, puts a finger up to rub her nose. The deepest lines around her eyes lift mysteriously and from under the bed she brings out a flute. Didn't I sweep under there this morning and find nothing?

She is like an owl, my old grandmother. Full of hoots and tricks, her eyes wide and alert in the dark of night. I do not always trust her.

"Grandmother! Where'd you get that?!" I reach to touch it. She swings it away. "it doesn't look like wood."

"It's not. It's made from the shinbone of a hawk, or so the carver said. You never knew with him, but I suspect it is bone." She brings it to her nose and sniffs it up and down, one way and then the other, eyeing me over its length.

"Although it could as well be a person's bone or a dog's bone as a hawk's. Now that I think about it, there was a man living way back in the woods, name of Ta-kuh-mo-say, who did show up lame around that time." She lifts her gaze from the flute and looks straight through me and out my backside, her eyes dark and bold, the film drawn up. She touches my hair, strokes a wisp of it back from my face. I draw back, guarded.

I don't know what she's trying to do. She's full of crap and nonsense again.

I watch her, watch her gaze slip sideways, travel off my face, the boldness draw back, see the tiredness fall into place. I push her hand from my hair, reach for the flute. But she quick lifts it high over my head.

"What is it, O-ko?"

But O-ko mes-se-maw is mimicking, uncannily and perfectly, the sounds of two completely different mating frogs.

"Okay, okay! So you're a frog. Or two frogs."

"Play it, play it for me, Child. Make those animals sounds you do so well."

"No, Grandmother," I say softly. "No."

"Play for me."

"No."

"Yes."

"No. You know I can play this flute, and I know I can play it. I've played other flutes, we know I can play it. Now, I am not going to play on command. Those are childish sounds; I don't do them any more. And quit bossing me around."

"Fine. Have it your way. I'll just die right now." And she keels over onto her side like a sailboat flat in the water, and lets her head roll off the pillow. Her tongue lolls out. A hoarse rasp comes from her throat. Then she is still.

---

I am not taken in.

"Good. Die in here so I don't have to hear your death rattle in the other room." I make motions toward the kitchen.

"There is a meaning for the person who receives the hawk bone flute." She eyes me determinedly from her side on the pillow.

"Grandmother!" I throw myself backward on the bed, arms and legs flung out in helpless resignation. I can't stand it any longer. "I don't want to be a member of the Midewiwin! They're all dead! The meaning is dead! Our symbols are dead. Dead, dead, dead. There's nothing!" I stop suddenly, embarrassed. How many "deads" did I say?

She sits up, wipes her mouth and rests the flute gently in her lap, her hands resting one over the other on it. I watch her hands, and the flute.

"They're starting it again, Sidney. They want us to be part of it, to bring back the old."

"And look where it got us! Dead!"

"Speaking of the dead, you should know it was your father who made that flute. Caught the hawk with a trap and a net. Killed it with his own hands, whittled the bone out, and brought it to me. 'Mother,' he said. 'Do you think my daughter would use it?' I don't know,' I said. 'You will have to ask her. It is not my place to say.' He wasn't only what you know he was, Granddaughter."

My breath leaves me like a shot expelled. Goes out the window and skitters across the ice sideways. The cold flings itself in through the hole my breath makes. I sit up suddenly and draw my legs tight against my chest. The ropes that are always around my heart from when Mama died and left me alone, before O-ko came and brought me here, tighten against the cold that floods in. I gasp for air and breathe snow. The stove! The stove has gone out! In my foolish fright, I am sure I have forgotten to put in more wood.

---

But, ah, no, I know better. It is that icy specter of my father rising soaked and bloated from the lake bottom, Death himself, stalking her, wrenching her from my arms, stealing the one person I have left to call mine.

O-ko mes-se-maw takes a harsh grip of my arm. I cling to her and can't let go.

"Now, my Granddaughter. You trap yourself," and she lets go of me so quickly I fall off the bed and land in a heap on the floor.

It is her death and his stranglehold.

Breathe in, breathe out. Don't let him in, Child. How can I stop him?

O-ko drops the flute on the bed and starts her weaving again, the loom clacking back and forth, back and forth.

I sit on the floor, unable to pull the blankets around me. My shivers are visible tremors, my knees literally bounce up and down. Has she become truly cruel?

She knows better. She was the one who came and got me out of the trailer. His death doesn't change that fact.

I lay my head against the end of the bed, exhausted, overcome, desperately in need of some small magic.

Well, maybe for old people there is magic just to be alive. And so. They deserve it, if they live long enough. But for me?

I remember when I was little, playing hide and seek in Mama's soft skirts and her rages at my father when he wasn't there to hear. We laughed and cried together, Mama and me, although I didn't know, really, at five or six or seven, what we were crying about.

Magic up and left me the night Mama died. I was nine. I remember waking stiff and sore from Mama's bed, O-ko lifting me, bundling me up and carrying me to her house through the deep snow, while my sister and brother struggled alongside holding onto her coat.

I remember seeing through the trees, the harsh winter

sun glinting off the ice and the fishermen moving here and there toward their shanties and the cold smell of the snow, and the wind just a ghost in the distance, an ancient voice receding into the hills.

I lie down on the floor, pull the blanket over my head. It is softer somehow down here. There's a muffle on the world.

I lift my fingers up and down, and pretend to play music on an imaginary flute.

When I was little I made a five-fingered flute from a hollow lake reed and created, exactly, the morning song of the Baltimore oriole, raced to play it for Mama that first time, while she stood, her hair braided long and pretty, hanging out clothes. She was so happy and surprised, she hugged me. She brought me my first real flute after that, and would often ask me to play something for her. "One of those animal sounds," she'd say. "Something pretty." Then she would sit smiling at the sky until I was done when she would give me a kiss and a bit of a sweet and go back to her chores, humming bits of my songs.

I spooked my sisters, playing the owl's hoot outside the trailer at night to scare them. They used to scream, then shout at me from the window, too scared to come chase me outside.

I play for tribal ceremonies now.

People say they feel whole and connected, listening. I'm not sure what they hear; it's hard to know.

Some say there is something sacred in the music. I don't know what "sacred" means. It's an odd word.

It is, perhaps, the memory of my mother, and in better days, my grandmother. I see them, loaded with fragrance, their arms filled with peppermint, crossing the long gold hill where the wind lays the tall grass down flat, the days, my family, as centuries, passing and returning on that hill, with the recurrence of skies untouched, the sun on their children's hair as the children scamper beside them. I play the morning eyes of a young husband seeing his wife brush her hair out with her fingers, as if for the first time, strand by strand, she soft and full of life.

How it could all turn out so wrong has nothing to do with the fact that in my mind, life, in some other time I never knew, once held magic in plain view of God.

I give them that. I can't seem to give it to myself. The music comes through me, and leaves me. It always seems to be for other people.

Who am I? I am the key of "A" on the flute, first, second and third finger, left hand. That's all I am. I can't stop Death, can't control things or even change them. I can't re-invent my own history. Can't re-invent theirs like Grandmother does in her weaving. I am not her.

But there are these times, when Grandmother's sleeping and her murmuring drifts off, I swear I hear Papa knocking on the door, the Death bear's icy claws scratching the wood to get in. I mean, of course, it's the cat clawing the top of the iron stove, or else it's my own fear ringing up in my ears. Still, I hear it, and it's not the wind, like Grandmother thinks.

I just wonder now, if she is stepping over onto this side or if she's still here on mine.

She finishes weaving and ties off the ends of the yarn.

I rise slowly, a little stiff in the knees. The flute lies silently on the bed, untouched, where she left it.

I fill my arms with wood for the stove, cram it all in and put my hands on the burners to feel the the heat come up. The warmth rises quickly.

The light outside is strong now, and I turn the wicks down in the lanterns, then off.

O-ko mes-se-maw has been leaning back against the bare wall. She sits up suddenly as I come in. I climb into the middle of the bed and sit cross-legged, facing her, our feud, if that's what it was, temporarily diminished. The bedclothes are messed up all around us, so I reach in front of her to straighten them out, ready the bed for her to go to sleep.

I am exhausted. She is still wide awake. I work around the flute and around her, tugging and pulling blankets and sheets until they are mostly neat. I can see, from the corners of my eyes as I work, that the flute is not made of bone, only ordinary wood, dry and cracked from age. Like her.

I haven't taken such good care of her. I often don't understand her and I let my own fears come in between us and fill up our special space. I don't like that. I start to cry.

O-ko stands up abruptly and knocks me completely off the bed onto the floor. This is it. Now comes the burst of energy, the lucidity, they say always comes just before death.

"I don't want you standing at my grave and crying." She leans over the edge of the bed, her hands on her hips, dark eyes fierce. "I won't be there."

And then she reaches down, lifts the flute, jumps off the bed, and runs out of the bedroom and through the back door onto the ice in her slippered feet. Quick as a wink. Startled, I run after her. Even the cat jumps up, its back arched.

"Out here!" she shouts. "He's out here!" She slides across the ice like a strange, running bird, her robe and gown flying behind her. The ice sparkles everywhere in the morning sun. I am utterly and completely blinded.

"What's out here, Grandmother!" I lose my footing and go down on my rump, spinning, right on the edge of one of the cracks.

I move on my knees over the crack, slip, and find myself with one foot in the icy water, my leg down in between the ice. I feel the suction on my foot from the lake and pull myself up quickly, trying not to twist my knee against the sharp edges of the ice. My leg is stuck.

I scream, scare myself, and stop. There is an odd elation

mixed with the sounds of fear in my throat, as if my own anger has found voice despite the fear, after all these years. It lets loose again, shrieking obscenities into the frozen air, all of them, everything, until the sound comes out empty, and my foot is resting on top of the ice again, my throat sore.

I don't see her until she is right on top of me, her face blue from the cold and deadly serious.

She reaches her hand deep down into the crack. Then her fingers uncurl, slowly, one at a time until the flute rolls out and splashes into the water. When I look down again, I see only a long slender shadow sinking slowly toward the floor of the bay.

Papa's not there, there's nobody there, nobody at all. No body or face, no human sound, no death hand knocking on the ice. There is only this — our two faces as we kneel, peering over the edge, reflected in the grey-blue of the bay down below, two deer, startled by the absence of anything at all.

For one second, she looks right into my eyes, the film drawn back, her gaze lucid as light, clear as the sun on a golden day. Then she grins, a big, huge, silly grin across her wrinkled little face, radiating from one side to the other, as if she has discovered a wonderful secret.

My own laughter is slow to come, a giggle, a chortle, then a full-throated, whole-bodied whistle with lungs straining as it gains momentum. I can't help myself, and roll over on my back, gasping for breath between each wave, until all I can say is, "Ungh, ungh, ungh," cackling like an old woman without teeth.

Her hands, bony but full of life and stronger than ever, reaching down, grasp mine and pull me up until we are dancing across the ice, first one way, laughing mercilessly, skipping and jumping, not even pausing for breaths, then back the other way, dancing, feather light.

My grandmother spins away, hopping from one foot to the other. She laughs a sing-song laugh, a startling, silvery, swept-up laugh that starts low and goes high like the Great Blue Heron lifting straight out of the water and into the sun, its huge wings shimmering blue and green. Her thin robe dances with her, flying up and down with each leap, until she is only billowy wings, rising with the warming breeze.

# THE NUMBER 6
# AND THE TOWN OF Y

In the twilight of morning, a wolf pack led by a she-wolf crossed the ice of Lake Michigan, arriving like strangers in need at the farmhouse door. Hearing their quiet *whoofing* breath in the snow, at the kitchen table, Stella lifted her pencil from numbers she couldn't make add up no matter how often she tried: the in-go, out-go, a balance that never rose above zero. At sixteen, she was the only one in the family who could read.

She dressed herself in her dead father's shirt, wool pants, and boots she stuffed with yesterday's newspaper, so she didn't have to spend money on clothes. Her mother had stopped asking her for a new coat after three months, and her brother, David, at fifteen, sat in his room rolling string around the floor, saying: *choo pa, choo pa*. And she couldn't figure out if he was saying *shoo pa, shoo pa*, because their father had drowned or, he was saying *choo pa, choo pa* because that's what their father said when he bought him a train set for Christmas three months ago.

She felt hunger in the air, heard something standing quiet at the kitchen door. Sometimes a cougar crossed the ice, other times wolves or elk, treading slowly, to see if the ice were sound.

Loss. That was what she felt, what the wolves brought.

Rising from her chair, she trod the creaking wood floorboards and pulled open the heavy oak door their father had cut and sanded last fall. Blue-eyed, rough-coated, they lowered their noses into the snow with a "schnuffing" sound. Looked at her.

She pulled the door to, crossed back beside the long wood table, past the wood stove for heating, and the iron stove her mother cooked on. Lifting a bowl from a shelf in the room where the wood was stacked, she padded back and tossed out squirrel entrails she'd saved from last night's meal. Nellie and Doll slept in the barn, and if wolves got hungry enough, there was no law that said work horses were not a suitable course for breakfast.

◆

"*Do* something with him!"

Her mother stood in the stairway door leading to the bedrooms above, lips pursed, hands clenched, snarled hair red as the sullen sun, which was not yet up along the rim of the bay. The sun would rise in the south, yawn, stagger north, sleepy in this cold country, and precisely at noon, hesitate, turn and begin its long trek home along the rim of the bay, pulling night over itself like a blanket, and not get up until next day noon.

A silk robe covered her mother's thin-boned frame, full of holes where moths had eaten through, threads ripped and hanging loose, a mere mask of a life unraveling. She had ridden here upstate, in her husband's new Ford car, sixteen years ago. But the car, too, now was sitting out on the back hill behind the barn, its tires flat, its green paint turning to rust by the constant storms the lake threw up. The house, itself, had worn out from six generations of children drawing on the walls, clothes the moths had eaten through in the closets, fences outside once strong and straight now leaning, as if the whole house wished to put its head down, tumble over the hill and be done with this life. It was crumbling now, its once bright paint peeling with age, its roof in need of re-shingling where the mice had gotten in and eaten every good thing: socks, doors, crackers, macaroni in the cupboards. Even the clothing they dressed themselves in wore out quickly as if to keep up with the rate of everything else that was falling and crumbling to dust with the house.

Stella glanced at the kitchen ceiling when her mother walked the floor in the upstairs rooms, shrieking that life wasn't fair.

She reached the second floor landing, swung around the corner at a gallop and stopped. Her hand went to her mouth, and tears sprang into her eyes.

"Stella?"

"David?"

"David."

"David!"

He fell over as she swung the door wide, the tail end of the rope that tied his hands to the door knob, swinging.

◆

He knew he wasn't supposed to climb Mama's dresser, but it smelled so *good* up there, like the pretty colors on the roses that grew in the garden. He remembered last summer Stella told him *not* to go into the old rose *garden* 'cause he might get ouchies! But Mama's dresser didn't *look* like an ouchie. It was red and pretty, so maybe it wouldn't *poke* him like Mama's garden *either.* He just wanted to smell that pretty smell. He pulled the bottom drawer out and wedged his dirty boot in there, pulled the next drawer out and climbed into it. He looked at the brown shoe print his foot left on Mama's frilly underwear, and thought what a pretty shape it made. Then he pulled open the next drawer And then, *bang!* that dresser fell over.

And now, at fifteen, he couldn't get his big fingers under the doorknob to untie the rope his hands were tied with. So he had waited, unable to call out, hands tied with a rag gagging his mouth which his mother pushed in to stop the noise, He waited, crying, slumped to the floor, wrists tied fast, until his arms grew tired, and then all he knew was that his arms hurt — a lot.

Downstairs, he heard Stella's voice raised: "You *tied* him to my...?" Thump-thumpthump, he heard, thump-thumpthump up the old wood stairs.

Loosening the knots, stroking his wrists where the shoelaces had rubbed his skin raw, she crossed into the bathroom and brought out a little jar from which she rubbed gooey softness over the places where the skin on his wrist had pulled away. Then it felt better. Pulling his big shoes over his feet, Stella laced them up, and tied loops in the laces. With each loop she told him a silly story about a letter of the alphabet.

"David?"

"Stella?"

"Do you know when the letter 'X' started to talk?"

"Before Y did," he said.

"Do you want me to read to you? Shall we do letters?"

He loved it when his sister sang his letters with him: A-a-a-a-a, she said. E-e-e-e-e, she pointed to her lips. I-i-i-i-i, she touched a finger to her chest. He clapped his hands.

She got up and went away, which made him sad, but then she returned with pencil and paper and drew funny little designs for him.

*Num-bers,* she said. *Let-ters. Es-s-s-s, tuh-tuh-tuh, oo-oo-oo.* And oh! He loved this. Clapped his hands. "'gain!" he shouted.

"Wait," she stood. "I'll be right back."

"No! Don't go!" He crawled across the hall and sat slumped outside the bathroom door. From inside she sang a song while he heard the sounds of water being poured into the metal tub. He listened to the uplift, the gentle skid down in her voice. Opening the door a crack, she looked at him. "You sing, too. *Loud* so's I can *hear* you in here!"

"Go down, -own! Moses-es-s-s. Way-ay down in E-e-e-gypt land-and-nd ... Tel-l-l-l ole, Phar-ar-oh-oh, to ... let-my-people-go-o ... " Though he knew little of the meaning, or the story she explained over and over, he never tired of hearing it.

Lost.

He felt like that Baby Moses most of the time.

"I'm getting into the tub," she shouted through the bathroom door. "You sing real loud so's I can *hear* you!" As she sang he was able to hum along with the sing-song chant with which she had taught him his numbers — the one she called "five," which looked like a cup with a hat on top, or the "six" with the tail that didn't go all the way around.

He cried over "six." He wouldn't say "six's" name. "One, two, three, four, five ... . seven!" he chanted angrily. And he left a pause, that little hole in the counting.

And through the bathroom door, she let him.

It had happened one day, when the leaves were deciding what color they wanted to be.

Sunlight wandered down through the tops of trees and slid down the trunks and oh, so-o-o-o slowly crept among the yellow and red leaves on the ground, like it was sneaking up on him. He played tag with the light, watching it stop and settle on the plant she called Fern, or drift over and sit quietly on the one she called Jack, or dangle off the plate-like mushrooms that stuck out from the bark of fallen logs, where sometimes she placed things from the forest he could eat.

"Remember what those plants look like, David, so you'll have something to eat if you ever get lost in the woods."

"What's *lost,* Stella?"

"It's when you don't know where you are."

"I'm here now."

"You sure are."

Sometimes, the light would follow him.

"When it touches you," she said. "That's when you are blessed."

"B-les-sed," he said. "What a funny name for the light."

"I can see you from the window up there," pointing to the house. "You come get me if you need to. Or shout up to that window and I'll hear you."

"Okay, Stella."

The light crawled over to him. Oh! How slowly! How he waited and waited and *waited* for it. He wondered what happened when you were blessed. It sounded scary, but Stella told him it was okay *not* to be afraid; and if Stella said it was okay, then it was O-kay.

Brushing his hands over the ground, he turned over a leaf and saw a squirrel sleeping. And yikes! There it was! The tail that didn't go all the way around!

"Six!" he shouted. "Stella! It's Six!" Scrambling to his feet, he picked up the squirrel by the tail and half-stumbled, half-ran through the basement door, up and up the stairs into the bedroom where Stella was tucking the corners of a sheet under a mattress. There he laid the squirrel on the bed, and very gently brushed his hand over its cold curled tail.

---

"It's Six, all right," said Stella, poking it. "You wait here." Coming back with a newspaper, she laid the stiff squirrel on the newspaper, rolled it up and tied it with a string. "Poor Six," she said. "Six is dead. We'd better bury him so he can go to squirrel heaven. Wait. I'll go change my slippers."

Their mother poked her nose in. "What's in that newspaper, David? What have you done now?"

Picking up the paper with Six inside, he hugged it to his chest. "Six!" he shouted. "It's Six!"

"Let me have it, you fool." Prying his fingers up one by one, she yanked it from him and accidentally dropped it onto the newly-made bed where it bounced on its head.

"It's dead! You stupid fool!"

"No! It's Six! It's the number Six!" He started to cry.

"Did Stella say you could bring this into the house?"

"Yes," he said. "So we can *bury* him."

He followed his mother's shoes tap-tapping down the stairs, stumbling, crying behind. Opening the back door, she hurled the number Six into the woods.

"Six!" he shouted. "You've thrown out the number 'Six'!"

"What's he talking about!" Their mother turned to Stella, who had come up behind.

"You've thrown out the number six," Stella said, folding her arms and lifting her chin. "It was a squirrel with a tail that didn't go all the way around."

"That's dumb."

"No. It's the way I *taught* him. So he *remembers*."

"*Remember*?! How is he supposed to learn anything if he always has *you*, getting him out of every single problem he gets into. How's he's going to grow up, if you keep coddling him? He's fifteen! Stop *babying* him!" And she bustled away, her shoes tap-tapping angrily on the stairs.

And that's how "six" got lost. Now, when he sang his numbers, he sang "five," skipped "six" and sang "seven."

And Stella let him leave that pause in the song of numbers, just as long a pause as he wanted.

◆

"David, you like Nellie-horse, don't you?" Stella asked. He nodded. "And *she* likes *you.*"

"Nellie Horse *likes* me," he said.

"I know she does, because she does what you tell her."

David nodded his head again.

"You went to Edmundsen's lumber mill last year and the year before that and the year before that, because Dad wanted you and Nellie to know the way, in case anything happened to us."

"Papa's in the cemetery."

"Yes, he is.'

"He's dead."

"Yes."

"Can you hitch Nellie to the ice boat and drive her across the ice to Edmundsen's lumber mill this morning, like you did last year, and the year before that? Remember how Dad taught you to do that?"

"Why?"

"Because Mom and I have to get the machines oiled and tuned up for spring planting now. The tractor needs a new tire and the man is coming today. And the sap is running now and we need to change the sap buckets. They're full and they'll spoil and we won't be able to sell them if the sap spoils."

"Mom can't go?"

"No. She's waiting for a man to come and fix the spray hose on the tractor, so it will be ready when the snow melts in a week or two. He only comes to this area once a year."

"Where's Dad?"

"In the cemetery. That's where he sleeps now, all the time. He caught pneumonia."

"Caught Nu-mone-yah. I remember, Stella. Can Nellie go?"

"Nellie-horse has gone every year for sixteen years and she knows the way." Stella stepped into her room and closed the door, leaving a crack. "Do it just like you did last year."

"Why?"

"Because Nellie likes you. She always does what you tell her."

"But why?"

"Because we need new buckets for the maple syrup trees."

"Why?"

"And eight six-by-fours to patch the holes the raccoons made in the sap boiling shack."

"Why?"

"Because I can't go this year; because I broke my foot in the fall from the hay loft and it's not healed yet."

"Why?"

"So we can buy groceries."

"Groshees ... "

"Shall we memorize the list together in a little song? You can sing it out to Mr. Edmundsen like you did last year. Remember?"

"Doll won't go?"

"No," she said. "Doll-horse needs to stay in the barn. She's got a cracked hoof."

"Will Nellie go?"

"If you ask her nicely."

"I always ask nicely, Stella."

"You've gone to Edmundsen's lots of times. When you're done just follow the horse home. She knows the way. Just like last time."

"Just like last time, Stella." And David smiled proudly.

She told him to put on his winterest clothes. Downstairs, she stuffed his pockets full of dried tomatoes and beans she'd hung in the attic to dry eight months ago last summer.

"I don't like beans," he said.

"You eat them when you're out on the ice."

"Don't yell, Stella."

"I'm not yelling."

"It sounds like you are."

◆

*Bang!* Those barn doors thundered in the wind.

"Hey, sno*w!* Who said *you* could come in, huh? You take that snow out, *right now! You hear?! You dummy! Coming in with your boots on. Didn't I tell you?!"*

*Clump-clump* went his boots down the old wood stairs. Doll lifted her brown chin over the stall door, and whinnied softly.

"Nellie's coming back, Doll. I *geewhiz doublethinkso.*" He stood in front of Doll's stall, stroking her brown ears. Over the stall wall, Nellie nodded her head, up and down. "Nellie-Belly! Go for a walk?" Lifting the latch to Nellie's stall, he looped a lead rope over her ears and swung the door out on its hinges. *Creak.*

*Click-click, click* went Nellie's iron shoes — *thump-thumpthump* over the old wood floor.

"Hey now! Whoa. Stand *still.*"

Seventeen hands high, weighing 1300 pounds, Nellie nosed his pockets, goosed him in his behind, tugged a blue kerchief from his pants and waved it up and down, like she'd just won a prize at the county fair.

"You're a *coyote* of a horse!" he murmured. "A goof! Does *Doll* ever ask me for anything. No-o-o-o-o. But you! You'll get me in trouble one day, Miss Nellie. What if somebody *else* is taking you across the ice. Huh? What'll you do *then?*" And he felt better for calling her names, cursing her out in a gentle sing-song. Because what did she know?

*Nothing.* That's what.

He held out his hand.

She shook her head.

"Fine. *You* tell Stella you don't want to go to the lumber-yard."

Outside the barn doors, snow fell softly now, thickly, covering the road, hiding the house from view.

Nudging his rear with her nose, Nellie bobbed her head up and down. "Oh, so *now* you've changed your mind. You want to *goose* me. Well, I'm not goosing *you*, Miss Nudgy-Nudge. You smell bad back there. You're pe-yooey."

The lower barn doors creaked open, and Stella stepped in. Pushing the barn doors wide, taking hold of Nellie's bridle, she led her around the corral and through the gate to the ramp where the ice boat sat, four inches of snow lining its traces. In a feint — to the right! to the left! — she snatched the kerchief from Nellie's mouth, tossed it up, snapped it down and handed it to David who tucked it in his back pocket, leaving one blue corner gently blowing in the wind.

"Go the way Nellie knows!" Stella shouted words that David couldn't quite make sense of in the wind ... "thicker in the middle ... careful near the shore."

"Careful," David said. "Shore."

"Sing out to Edmundsen what I taught you, David! Sing it out real LOUD! So he can *hear!* He's near deaf!"

His mother said don't be loud. David didn't like people mad at him. What was she so mad about all the time, anyway? He'd sing it out softly, in case his mother heard, so she wouldn't get mad.

"I'll make you a chocolate cake when you get back, David!"

---

"You better, Stella!"

"Johnny Reb, Johnny Reb's horses all come along, come along-g-g!" Using the song his father had taught him when he and Nellie were smaller, David sang out the rhythm he wanted Nellie to pick up in her stride: "1-2, 1-2, Johnny Reb, Johnny Reb, you can't beat the Blues! 3-4, 3-4, pick your feet *up, Nellie, pick 'em up high!*" Nellie flicked her ears back toward him. She *liked* his songs. It didn't matter if his mother said horses didn't know words. *He* liked them and the *horse* liked them. And if Stella said they were okay ... then they were *okay.*

Nellie lifted her head and swished her tail, walking in a high trot as if she were a high bred Thoroughbred set to win a big race at the state fair. Stella smiled at David, slapped Nellie's rump, and tramped back over the path in the snow she'd made over the road to the house. *Scrape, scrape,* her shovel went on the old porch steps. *Scrape, scrape.*

The snow parted briefly. On the front steps, resting her chin on the shovel handle, his sister lifted a red mitten in return. David danced a funny little gait. Turning round, Stella bent over and showed him her bottom. David slapped his hands to his backside in mock astonishment, as if to say he didn't know girls HAD bottoms.

Crossing the ice to Elk Rapids, loading lumber on for the maple sugar shed, he sang out to Edmundsen to also throw on several pounds of sawdust for cleaning the horse stalls. Oh, and why not add on that bucket of nails his mother had asked for that David had forgotten last time? And *oh!* He almost *forgot!* He needed 40 potato crates of the heavy wooden kind. The ones Mr. Edmundsen sold him last year didn't last. The slats fell off and the the bottoms rotted out.

"Slats," David said. "Bottoms," he sang. "Rotted." And he sang the words out now, the way Stella had taught him, in a song. "You *like* songs," she'd said. "Sing it out when you get to Edmundsen's. So's you'll remember."

◆

A.E. Edmundsen had a caved-in chest, greasy red hair, a face marked by black broken teeth and a nose bent to one side as if someone had clamped pliers on and turned it clockwise.

Onto the sled, Edmundsen threw up sap buckets with no handles. Rusted nails. Lumber sent back for cracks.

"Broken," David's hand touched a handle hanging off a bucket. When he got down to check the horse's harness, Edmundsen took the bucket off with a great deal of grunting and swearing under his breath, and quietly threw it back on.

"Buckets?"

"Buckets."

"Wood?"

"Wood."

"Ice hold?"

"Still holding, kid." Into David's pocket, he tucked a bill of sale, which he scribbled off in a dash and didn't bother reading to the boy. What for? When the boy wouldn't know what it said anyway? Then maybe his sister, Stella, would come by boat next fall, and pay him once the potato crop came in. *If* the potato crop came in, it *never* came in. Then he'd open those tight lips of hers, and maybe open something else, too. Give himself a bonus. Brown broken teeth flashed as he slipped his tongue in and out.

"Sign your 'X' here, son, and put the paper inside your coat pocket." He swung around and slapped the next customer on the shoulder. "Hey, there, Will-yard DeGraw! What can I do you out of today?! That wife of yours found a handsomer fellow to eat her strawberry pie?"

◆

Nellie lowered her head into the weight of the sled. The creak and scrape of iron crossing ice. Snow fell like handkerchiefs, ice milk, hard nuggets of silver. The wind drove down, turned and screeched across the ice, its lone voice echoing back, echoing back.

Perhaps he shouldn't have taken the horse across the ice; but if he went around by land, he'd be *two days* going home. Stupid kid! his mother'd say.

No.

He'd go the way he knew.

But ice doesn't tell where it's weak. Looking out across the surface of the water five miles or more, it all looks flat and clean and safe. Light shining on it blinds the eyes so as not to ask: where's it solid, where's it weak? Where do ripples start up, water steam through? Where is it warmer beneath the ice than on the surface? When does it break apart and slam together again, until it *booms* in broad daylight, creating seams where, if you mapped the ice's surface, the topography would be different today than yesterday, *now* than an hour ago?

David was only over twelve feet of water, thirty yards from the home shore, when the first sled runner cracked through the ice. Under the weight of a 1300 pound work horse and a ton of wood logs, it went down with the speed of light; it just *seemed* to happen slowly, at the moment the crack rippled open like a fissure.

Stacking jelly jars on the porch, Stella heard a long-drawn out howl she thought was the first hint of a gale coming across the lake.

Out on the ice, the wolves lifted their voices. They knew the ice; they knew what it wanted, and what it wanted it would *take*. In intimate song, their throats rose in crescendo, calling and calling, until the wind and the howls slammed together, opening the wounds of grief.

With the weight of the logs, each thick round as a barrel, the sled rose on end, tipping David and the horse in through a crack which widened, grew wet, deepened then split. Sawdust and nails skittered across its breaking surface. Boxes fell, spilled, broke open. Seams opened beneath the stone boat, growing wider, like a tidal pool the water rips up, starting with a tiny fissure, widening to a river, then a pond so great one *can't* climb out.

It was then that her name rose to the air.

"Stel-l-l-l-a-a!"

On the porch, she lifted her head and turned toward the ice, her name shouted like terror on the wind. Fear struck her heart, grasped it with the muscle of a man's working hand and wrenched it out of her chest. She saw the wolves on the ice, tails down, voices lifted in a howl so mournful, she knew disaster had come.

Darting across the snowy road, flying past the barn she plunged down the cliff path in deep snow, following David's track. Racing after, her mother yanked her flailing arms and legs out of the snow, bound her down to the child's sled she'd snatched to fetch her. Tied her arms down.

Dragged her back.

Shrieking and kicking and clawing: Lemme go! *Let-me-go!*

But her mother slapped her hard.

Where were you going, little fool?

*Any* ice would have cracked.

53

Stella stood on the porch waiting, noting the soft hum of spring bees in the trees where the wild cherries grew. Waited, feeling she wanted to go look at those bees. Perhaps it was time to switch to a new crop; potatoes had worn out the land, growing smaller and punier each summer that passed, until they were mere nuggets that people passed by in the farm markets, and did not buy.

A fancy horse and carriage pulled up: gold plate on the side, fine leather, new wooden wheels. Then the magistrate was there, talking to her, but it was like he was talking through the wrong end of a bullhorn, because she couldn't hear him.

"My apologies," she said. "I - I don't believe I heard you ... ? He isn't there . . ?"

"Your brother's not there, miss."

"My brother's not ... where?"

"Where the stone boat went down."

"What do you mean he's not where the stone boat went down? He was standing on it when it went through the ice. He *has* to be there." She took the hat off with the brim that shaded her eyes, and turned to look down the cliff road to the lake. The ice had broken up and was drifting on open water. A light spring rain fell, slowly, softly.

Accustomed to repetitive questions from those who have lost family members, the magistrate waited. When she did not speak, he spoke simply, clearly. "There is no sign of your brother. No clothing, no body."

"No ... ? Body? You're saying my brother's body is not in the water where he went through the ice last winter? What was that red shirt we saw through the ice? Wasn't it a shirt? Didn't you see that red shirt when we looked through the ice?"

"You may have seen a refraction of the sun."

"Sun? I work outside every day in potato fields, next to that lake. You think I don't know how sun refracts on ice?"

He stood quietly, hat in hand, head down, respectful of loss.

"And Nellie?"

"Nellie?" He looked at her blankly. "Oh, your horse. Right. The horse is not there, either. The divers found only the stone boat."

"But ... "

"I can only guess that the horse may have swum out, if the ice was soft enough to break up. But there's no indication where. Or in what direction. Without tracks, I can't tell you which way he went to get to shore. And whether or not your brother was with him."

"Her."

"Her?"

"The horse is a her."

"My apologies. Her."

"And my brother, David?"

"Your brother, I am sorry to say, is missing."

"Missing?"

"Yes."

"It is a better report than dead," Stella said.

◆

It seemed all night the great horse slipped through the water, her powerful legs pushing forward, her great chest heaving as the ice rammed against her sides and swirled away in currents, sending rivulets of blood streaming out behind.

Her old frayed harness broke, snapped, fell away. The stone boat drifted down, lumber and buckets tumbling through the waves, sinking in to the muck, which rose in a cloud that colored them with a grey that hides all things that drown.

It is not known how long it took for the horse to tire, or when it was that her hooves struck bottom; it may have been all night she swam through the dark water. Perhaps there were tracks where she came out, hoofmarks hardened by ice and snow in the frozen sand, so that if Stella found that place, if she had been there and looked down, she would have seen it, for she knew how to track an animal. You do it the same way you track the great wolf or a fox, a wild turkey or the ring-necked pheasant, for in the stark reality of winter, the only way to keep from starving is to learn what the winter teaches.

Nellie tripped over rocks at the water's edge, scraped her knees tiredly against boulders that lined the unfamiliar shore. As their size did not allow her to step over them, she stepped around them, nostrils flaring, ears twitching, listening for the sounds of men.

The Percheron was a horse bred to be of service to people, a horse whose heart bled deep into the land. Raised in kindness, strength and duty, trust and work were all she knew.

Around great boulders she stumbled now, through a forest of blue spruce and great northern pine, led by duty and instinct, and a powerful sense that more was being asked of her than she usually gave. She had a great desire to find people, for people padded felt beneath the leather straps when she pulled heavy loads, laid hay in her manger before her morning's work, and at night let her lay down in clean straw. A work horse, work and kindness were all she knew.

In the evening, spring tiptoed in, leaving tiny tracks in the snow from chipmunks' small footprints, moles running askance through the underbrush. On the tall maples, tiny green nodules appeared overnight that might or might not transform themselves into leaves. High up in a beech, an eagle brought the first branch to her nest, where the snow dripped onto the hats and shoulders of the men below.

Arms and chests the breadth of the old-growth trees, they were men of great strength, who had spent their winter in a lumber camp owned by Perry Hannah, who had hired teams of men to clear-cut the forest. Open ground lay studded with stumps where once the great trees stood. Along the river, a sawmill cut the logs and floated them down down river.

"Aye, and away, men! There'll be no tomfoolery today! Every man to his tree! Let's see ye work as if ye were still on board the Catalina raising the topmast and slip! I know ye remember it well, for I was leadin' ye then and I'm leading ye now. And if ye don't like it, ye can sign onto another lumberman's camp, and be worked to death with no food like other men's crews." He took from his pocket a whistle that blew so loudly, the leaves on the great maples seemed to shiver and hum to its call.

In snow-covered tents, along the banks of the river, beneath the great jack pines and blue spruce, huddled in their blankets, the lumbermen slept, dreaming the dreams of men whose work has left them without the company of women: fingers to run through their hair, hands to spoon steaming food in their mouths, legs and arms to take them to bed and warm them in the late winter air, conversations about music and culture, singing, poetry, things they themselves knew little of. There was only one woman in this camp, the 10-year-old assistant to the cook, a bristly old man with a hard paunch, tattoos on his arms of ships and serpents, and a cigar he never lit plugged into his jaw. And while he cursed the slowness of the fire, for the wood was wet this morning, she nipped two pieces of venison from the frying pan, dropped them into her waistband and ran. Eliza, she was called, an Indian girl, though she never answered by name, for she had never told them her real name, or that she was

Odawa Indian, or that she was not deaf. A sly one, she had hidden a week's worth of food in her blankets, stolen from the cook's tent. Nightly during the poker game, she ghosted in, nipped bread left warming on the stove, cut venison with her knife that the cook left drying on a string from a pole and tucked it in her pockets and ran.

Walking among the cots now, tapping his cane against knees and elbows, the foreman's voice rose deep and strong, piercing the men's raw dreams.

"There'll be no tomfoolery today, men! It's hard work until the forest is cut! Ye'll work as if we were still on board the Catalina, raising the topmast and sail. Ye'll remember the Great War, for I was leading ye there, and I'm leading ye still, and if ye don't like it, ye can just go without work and food like everyone *else* in this country!"

Grunting and groaning, lifting their blankets from the ground and rolling them neatly — because the Quaker insisted on a clean camp — they stumbled around the thick trunks of trees to do what was necessary, sitting briefly on heels and haunches, watching the cook flare up the fire banked against last night's wind, sniffing rabbit and venison for the noon meal, gruel and black coffee for the morning.

With the crackle of branches, they reached for their rifles. Working in the forest made them sensitive to sound: the hesitant step of a doe — food, the way a wolf walks like a dog — danger. Once fighting men in the Spanish-American War, they knelt, lifted their rifles, drew back their hammers. Took aim.

Crackling through the trees, chest the size of a schooner's prow, Nellie trudged into the clearing, head down, dripping, stumbled to a halt and fell to her knees.

"Jesus, God and Mother Mary! Hold yer fire!"

How she understood where they were we never knew, for the horse had crossed ten miles through the water, the

58

boy's fingers wound so tightly into her tail, the old Quaker, exhausted by age and work, could not yank them free. Rising, cursing, striding quickly to his cabin, sharpening his hunting knife on a whetstone, he bolted a quick breakfast of fried squirrel he'd shot yesterday, banked his small fire to burn all day, and strode back to the boy. Crossing his short stout legs, pulling the horse's tail into his lap, he cut the long strands of her tail out where it was laced deep into the cracks and crevices of the boy's hands.

"The rest of ye to work!" The men scattered to their saws and ropes, harnessing the lumber horses, urging the logging wagon deeper into the forest, along a scrape of ridge beside the lake where there was no track and a trail had to be hacked through. Through the trees came the sound of the rhythmic scrape and grind of saws on wood. A shout rose. A single grand elm began to dance and sway, shake its top, whisper, lean and fall, its reverberation shaking the earth with the sound of God and Satan fighting underground.

Crouched beside the boy at the fire who was wrapped in blankets borrowed from the men, the old lumberman praised the horse who stood next to the sleeping boy, crunching hay. "Aye, ye did good work, old girl, I compliment ye. You're a hardy one, but where in the Sam Hill ye come from, I haven't a clue. Cain't ye talk a bit and tell me, where the boy's folks are?" But the horse just crunched the hay the old man gave her, gazed at him with her tired brown eyes, and nodding her head, exhausted, her work for the boy done now, sloped to the ground. Front legs first, back legs buckling, she rolled onto her side and closed her eyes.

The Quaker rose and walked quickly to his cabin. Striding the dirt floor to the fire's hearth, he lifted heavy scissors he kept sharpened and cleaned on a nail, picked up a pail of water he might have used to boil his morning tea, stalked off to the cook's fire, returned with a bucket of oats, placed the oats and water before the horse, knelt between the horse and the boy, and, one by one, tugged the long matted hairs of the horse's tail from between the boy's fingers, hardened and stuck together with drying blood, then cleaned his shears with water from the bucket, dried them thoroughly, rose once more, trod to the makeshift cabin and placed them back on their nail on the hearth. Leaning down once more, he grasped one arm beneath the boy's knees, one behind the boy's neck, and hefted him up with effort, for he was an old man who had once been strong. But though his muscles had withered with age, he still carried the trained endurance of a sea captain who once led soldiers to war; and with an upward thrust and buckling knees, he staggered to the rough cabin, laid the boy on a bed of soft green pine, pulled the wet shirt and pants off of him, took a blanket from his own roll, laid it over him, reached up on a shelf, took a second blanket for himself, unrolled it on the hard packed floor, and reaching in with a stick, banked the fire to burn all day. If the men needed questions answered, they knew where to find him.

"S-stella?"

The old man rose onto one elbow and retrieved his pipe from a small shelf below the window, packed it with tobacco from a leather pouch, clamped it in his teeth, and lay down, then rose and turned and leaned over and pulled a stick from the fire, laid it against the pipe tobacco, and lay down again, propping his head up on his arm.

"S'ella?" The voice was hoarse and weak.

"There is no S'ella here, son." The Quaker rose from the blanket on the floor, nudged another log into the fire, poked at it with a poker, stood and walked out, brought snow back in, scooped it into a metal pitcher and set it on the fire to boil.

"Do you know the letter 'Q'?" The words whispered out.

The old man peered into the kettle, seemed satisfied for a moment, then rose and laid more wood underneath it from kindling stacked in three neat stacks by the door: small to start the fire, medium for cooking, and large cut logs for a hot fire. With the fire started, he placed a large cut log on. Squatting on his haunches, he nudged another stick into the flames and sat back, rubbed his chin, and said to the boy, "Yessir, I believe I have on occasion met the letter 'Q'."

"Q has a tail."

"Ah, ye know your letters, do ye? Better than most me men out there who can't spell much more than their names."

"I-i-i-i-i-e-e-e-e," the vowels whispered out hoarse and raw.

"Aye. Can ye count then, too?"

"One, two, three, four, five, seven, eight, nine, ten," the boy coughed weakly.

"Now, let me see here. One, two, three, four, five ... seven? Do ye think there's a number missing, son?"

"Yes sir," the boy whispered. "It's a number where the tail doesn't go all the way around," and he coughed, a deep raw racking from his chest.

"Drink your tea, now. Let's see here, a number where the tail doesn't go all the way around, ye say?"

"Yessir."

"Well then, it would have to be six or nine, wouldn't it?"

"Six!" the boy shouted hoarsely. "Six!" And he slapped his knees until the old man, too, laughed, rocking back and forth in merriment.

"Aye, we're two peas in a pod, boy. I'll enjoy your company while you're here, but I 'spect your people will be wanting to find ye soon."

"Find," David said.

"Aye. If ye mean the horse, she's sharing my own horse's hay and oats. Did ye know notice ye wound your fingers into her tail so tight I had to bandage your hands?"

"Ban-dij?"

"Aye, boy. Those wraps on your hands."

---

"Hands," David said, turning them back and forth. "White," he said.

"Aye. And ye'd best leave 'em alone until they heal. Then we'll see about getting those bandages off."

"Heal?"

"Aye. Heal."

"Aye?" But David drifted once more into dreams, pulled through the waves, thrashing with his feet to keep his head above water, winding his fingers into the long tail of the horse, until the strands couldn't easily come undone. The exhausting work of holding on had tired him, and then even his head went down, and he slept.

◆

Light snuck in quietly through the cabin window and slid across the floor. Oh! so slowly! that light came in, round and yellow and small. How it crept around the room. Outside he heard noises, and somewhere far away a person laughed.

"Sleep," David said. "Dark now." He didn't remember what he was supposed to do. "Dark," he said. "Sleep?" But he didn't.

*Thump-thumpthump* he heard. There! Rubbing against the inside wall. White! Like a ghost!

"Go away, Ghost!" he yelled, and pulled the blanket up to his chin. "I'm not here. You go away, Ghost!"

Pushing the door open, it put its wet nose on his hair and sneezed, for Nellie had simply nudged the cabin door open with her nose and clumped in.

"Funny," he said. "You have whiskers just like Dad, Nellie."

Sneezing once more, for she had gained a bit of cough in the water, Nellie lowered herself onto her knees, hind legs buckling, front legs folding, and dropped to the floor, rolled over on her side, laid her big head in his lap like a dog, and sighed.

He sang a little song for her, about a horse and a boy who were friends, and then, tucking himself into her warm belly, slept.

Sunlight wandered down through the leaves of the trees and crawled across the open door, and Oh! so slowly! climbed up the blanket and pounced on his chest, where it jumped to his arm and then to his head, where it perched in his hair.

"What are you doing, Sun?" David mumbled, sleepily, reaching up to pat the sun on his head that streamed in through the dirty window.

"Aye, there, Son. It's good to see ye awake."

"Awake?" David said hoarsely, and turned his head, slowly, to see who spoke. His head hurt a *lot*.

"I see your horse sorely missed ye, boy."

"Nellie?" His voice whispered.

"She is indeed, son, out munching hay with the other horses at this moment. I shooed her out."

"Do you know about the letter 'X'?"

"The letter 'X'? Is that near the town of 'Y'?"

"Yessir," David said. "The town of 'Y'."

"Will ye be wanting coffee, Mr. X?"

David shook his head side to side vigorously and sat up.

"And will Mr. X's horse be drinking water?"

"Yessir, Nellie likes to drink water."

"Good. I'll tell the boys to make sure she gets taken down to the river for water with the other horses."

"Are you God?"

"Nossir," the Quaker chuckled. "I'm a Quaker turned lumberman, son, the foreman of this unit. And if ye're smart ye'll never confuse me with God."

"Kway-ker," David said softly. "Lum-bear-man."

"That's right. A Lum-bear-man. That's what I am." And he laughed and patted his round tummy. "You like tea?"

"Yessir."

"You're very polite. Where ye from, son?"

"Stella."

"Is that the name of your town?"

"Town?"

"The address ye live at." David sat up, worried, then gazed hard into the burning fire. "Ye have people, son?"

"Stella said there were things in the woods I could eat if I got lost, and when the light sat down on me, I'd be blessed."

"Ye *assuredly* are blessed, son, to survive that icy water over that distance. Although we don't really know from where ye came. Are ye from the side of the bay that raises potatoes?"

"Stella knows what dandelions are called, and cherries, and apples, and even ants. She can tell you that. You'd have to ask *her*."

"Aye, so ye do know cherries and apples."

But the boy was quiet, eating the bread the Quaker had given him.

"Do you remember what the house you live in looks like?"

David was quiet for a moment. "White," he said.

"Aye. White. Like 99% of the houses in this country. We'll have to think, son, how to get you home. I've laid some of me own spare clothes for ye beside your blanket. Get dressed, and when ye're ready, go down to the cook, and have him give ye a few spoonfuls of gruel, like the men who work get. If ye can walk and talk, ye can earn yer keep same as the rest of 'em. No work, no food. Understand?"

"Yessir. No Work. No Food. That's what Stella says."

"Good, I hope to meet your Stella, one day. She sounds like a fine person."

"Here!" With a rolled cigar in his mouth he never lit, a mermaid tattooed on his stomach the size of a wooden barrel and legs thin as dandelion weed, the cook reached into a pot hanging over the fire, scooped gruel into it, and handed David a bowl. "You hungry, boy?"

"Hungee...?" But the bowl the cook offered David shook so hard in David's hands, the spoon did a little dance against the sides of the bowl and popped out onto the ground.

"What's the matter with you? You got palsy, boy? Polio? The flu took some o' the men last month. You ain't got the flu now, do y'? The small pox's already swept through here, and took three. The boss was swearing in Quaker then."

Famished, starved, lifting the bowl to his lips with shaking hands, letting it slop down his chin, wiping his mouth with his sleeves, David tipped the bowl up and sucked in the gruel like it was mother's milk.

"You could teach the men to be appreciative of my cooking. Ain'tcha got no coat, boy?"

David's eyes left the bowl he had put to his mouth in hunger, and looked down.

"Lost your tongue, son?"

David said nothing, but nodded. His trembling seemed like it would carry him up in to the clouds, he shook so ferociously.

"The girl, Eliza, will take care of you. She can't be babysitting you all day, she's got chores. But she'll help y' with what y' need. What's your horse's name, boy?"

"Nellie," said David.

"Nellie," said the cook. "That horse of yours done drug you a long ways! And through the water! He's some horse."

"She," David said.

"She," said the cook, admiring Nellie, who was eating hay. "The Quaker's going to put you to work, boy. We need everyone we can get. Mr. Hannah wants 30,000 ton of logs runnin' downriver by midnight."

"'annah?"

"Boy, I don't ask the boss his business and you'd better not either. Don't go asking things you don't know nothing about and you'll get along fine." David nodded his head up-and-down three times, like Stella had taught him when he answered questions from his mother. *Just nod,* she'd said.

He nodded.

"Good. The Quaker lost one man from pleurisy yesterday, and he needs someone for the sawmill crew who's got strength. From looking at you, I'd say you're the right fellow. Get up and get yourself down to the river and ask the Native girl, Eliza, for a second pair of pants and a shirt. We're going to use that horse of yours, too. Hurry up!"

David ate, famished. The Native girl, Eliza, came and squatted beside him, hands on her knees, black hair short around her face in a ragged cut, watching as he placed the bowl to his mouth, slurping the gruel in, letting its contents run out the sides of his mouth, wiping the backs of his hands with the ragged remains of his sleeves. He rose, trembling, legs weak and buckling, but pulled himself up and stood tottering. The girl, Eliza, handed him a shirt and pants with boots on top, and left.

The sun shone through a clear space in the canopy of thick branches overhead, and for a brief moment he looked up as that ray of light passed over. And then he looked down upon the ground on which he stood.

"I am blessed," he said.

"Aye," the Quaker said, standing before him now, the cook stirring several pots behind. "You are indeed, son. Come along now. I've let ye rest; now it's time to earn yer keep. We'll see how much ye can do with yer strong arms."

"Stella?"

"Ye don't talk to these men about a woman, boy. They ain't seen a grown woman in months. We're loggers, working for the Perry Hannah Lumber Company out of Traverse City, and ye are big enough to do some lifting. Come on, ye'll need some hard work and sweat to stop shivering. Find this boy some clothes!" he shouted to the men sitting before the open fire, finishing their coffee from tin mugs, their faces lined dark with the pitch that covered their clothes from the pines. They wore long underwear beneath their sailing men's shirts, and pants which widened at the bottom from their naval days. "We spent enough time dawdling this morning because of ye, ye might as well work and get paid the same as the next man. Hannah don't take no loafers in *this* camp. Ye'll start with the rest of the men, moving piles of brush, then move into heavier work tomorrow. That horse of yers is going to haul wood. He's built fer it."

"She," David said, as he stood up. "Her name is Nellie."

"She," the Quaker replied. "My apologies. Well, Miss Nellie Horse and Mr. No Name, let's fix ye up and put ye to work, until ye figure out how yer going to get yer horse home. What's yer age, son?"

"One, two, three, four, five ... seven, eight, ninety-ten, eleventeen."

"Ah. Ninety-eleventeen, it is, then. And so, yer not counting the number six?" And he let six little puffs of smoke rise up from his pipe.

"No sir."

"All right, then," and he stroked his small gray beard. "Well, now. I never liked the number nine, myself," and two puffs came out of his pipe one right after the other.

David, curious, looked up. "The number nine?"

"The number nine."

"It's not like six."

"It sure isn't," the foreman said. "The tail is upside down."

David looked up, startled, then opened his mouth and let a guffaw come out. Laughed and laughed. "Upside down!"

The men lifted their heads from the fire, glancing carefully at the foreman with the hard face they'd never seen smile, and the overgrown boy with the face of a foundling. Their own grizzled faces glowed in the morning light, wrinkled, as if they had always been old men, though the work tore their muscles and strained their shoulders, until they walked stooped and bent, although they weren't much more than sixteen or twenty-five.

"Yessir!" the Quaker laughed. "I always thought they couldn't think of a number for the space between Eight and Ten, so they got lazy and used the number Six, which they had used before, but turned it upside down and called it Nine."

"Nine!" shouted David and fell backwards, laughing, the two of them then, the boy who thought the Number Six was a squirrel with a tail that didn't go all the way around, and the Quaker, the foreman of a lumber camp, who thought the Number Nine was a cheap imitation of Six.

"Ye should know that most of these men here don't count either, not on their fingers and not out there in the world. This is the only job they'll do. No one else will have 'em. Misfits they are. And ye'll have to keep up with them, or we'll have to keep the horse and let ye go. Understand?"

David nodded his head fast and hard, nodded two more times, and counted both times to reach the number nine, and not once did he put the number six in.

A sharp neigh rang out, and David rose and ran toward it, the Quaker close behind. Two men were trying to harness Nellie to a heavy wagon loaded with logs. One struck her, and she reared.

"No! You have to do it *this* way," David said quietly. He took the reins from one of the men and, lengthening them, sang to Nellie in a soft sing-song until she reached around and pulled the blue kerchief from his rear pocket. He finished adjusting the buckles so they weren't too tight or too loose, all the while singing to her in his soft voice.

They set off at a slow walk, following the men, the blue kerchief dangling from her mouth, the men smiling. They slapped the boy on the back. David didn't stay in camp with the cook; he took hold of Nellie's halter the whole day, working beside her, backing her into the traces of the lumber wagon, adjusting her harness so it didn't rub her shoulders, urging her on under the weight of the logs.

"You're a strange one," one of the lumbermen said in the evening, as the glow of the men's campfire lit their faces orange and yellow in the darkness beneath the forest canopy.

"Do you know when the letter 'X' started to talk?" David asked.

The lumbermen smiled. "You tell us, boy."

"After 'Y' did!" And the men coughed and spit and dropped their spoonfuls of beans on the ground until the cook insisted they had to scrape them up and wash the dirt off themselves. Laughing loud and long, they slapped David on his back, until the beans came out of his mouth, and a little squirrel darted in, picked them up, stuffed its cheeks full and vanished up a tree.

◆

David slept in a group by the fire at night, and all day he worked, and all day Nellie worked beside him, the two of them gaining strength back daily. At night the men taught him how to cut wood for kindling, four ways to start a fire, why maple burns quicker than oak: start with poplar or maple, don't put oak on until the fire is burning because oak is slow to start, but it's thick and will burn all night once the fire's going strong. The ash trees, the men said, were all dying, and they showed him the ash borer and the hole it made in the trunk. They showed him how to cut a thin strip of wood from a long board and soak it in water overnight, so in the morning it could be bent to curl over spokes for a wheel. They taught him how to spit into the wind without it coming back on him. And how to write his name when he peed, and so he learned his alphabet, a new letter three times a day.

The days warmed up so that the men took their coats off, and left them in the camp. The forest leafed out again, little wisps of six-pointed oak leaves poking out overhead, and the clatter of Canadian geese returning to the northern sky, skidding on the surface of the lake they followed, returning from the south. And the May flower lifted its green and white striped head and shook its frail body in a fighting stance in the ever present wind that crossed the great lakes in a whirl.

"All right, men! Get ye'selves up and pick up yer belongings! We're moving today! Heading north, up river. Packs, saddles, horses, lumber wagon, saws and yer personal belongings. Perry Hannah's got no time for sluggards. Pack yer horses up, get yer gruel and coffee! Let's go, let's go! Ye men dilly-dally like little girls powderin' yer faces. A pretty lot ye'd be, too, with hair all over ye like bears! Put that fire out and move!"

With a great bustle of energy, they went to it. David watched what the other men did, and wrapped his few belongings — a watch whose fingers spun around, two undershirts the men had given him. His own tin cup for coffee, which the cook had given him, he tied on his belt with a little rope. And then he harnessed Nellie, and stood her in the line of other horses, hitched to the lumber wagon.

"Not this time, son. That horse of yours done needs a rest. We been working 'er real hard these last weeks, and she's done real well. She deserves a break. Let her walk with ye, or ye can ride 'er, if ye wish. She can pull some of the crates and boxes the men made, along with the lumber. They're lighter than the lumber mill."

"Ride?" said David.

"Aye, ride, boy. Ye could probably sleep on her broad back. Go ahead. We'll let the other horses pull the lumbermill saw for a while."

"Okay, then," David said. The other horses, behind in their slow huge way, the men behind the wagon, their packs on their backs, the Quaker had him harness Nellie to the wagon of cut lumber and crates, and they moved forward, while David, on Nellie's wide back, with her slow pace at the front of the line, put his head down on her neck, wrapped his fingers in her mane, and on her wide back, slept.

"Wait!" The girl, Eliza, ran alongside. "Take this," and she handed him a little burlap bag the size of a wallet. "The foreman said it's time you got paid for your work. Seventy dollars."

"Thank you, miss," he said.

"You're welcome, sir."

Sir, he thought. I'm a sir. Perhaps "sirs" belong to the number 6. Sir Number Six. That's what he was.

◆

It was a long ways they walked, past dusk into night. The wind rose whispering. Trees beckoned, called, tossed their heads, flung their arms out. Branches arched, cracked, thudded on the ground. Above the swaying trees and the sheeting rain, the sky cried and raged. And when the wind howled and moaned, David, trembling, moaned, too, calling for Nellie. And rose in the night to see if she were okay, and saw nothing. The branch he'd tied her to had been snapped off, dragged through two trees and was stuck there. Only the frayed end remained, snagged between the split trunk of twin maples, their combined girth wider than the horse.

"Lost!" David yelled. "Nellie!"

He heard her neigh, and looked around wildly for her direction, but the thrashing of the trees was loud, and he couldn't see in the rain that had begun as a drizzle, then opened to a downfall and fell to a torrent.

"Take care of your horse, and your horse will take care of you." That's what his father had taught him. And he hadn't done that, had he? He hadn't tied the rope tight enough, his big fingers unable to get the knots right, and now Nellie was gone, wasn't she?

"Nellie!" he shouted.

David sat in the woods. "When all else fails, wait," he said. And as he laid his head on his arms and his arms on his knees, the soft brush of her lips touched his head. He swung around and grabbed her around the neck, climbed up on a stump, threw a leg over her back, and laying his head along her soft mane, slept, because like many other things he had learned, the men had also taught him how to sleep in the pouring rain. From the broad back of the horse, he would never lose her.

◆

The long night she walked, rain sheeting off her back, shivering when lightning stroked down, shuddering when the sky broke open in thunder. Shards of fire lit the darkness. Over and over the air cracked in great thundering claps, which broke and rolled through the sky like God and Satan fighting for the right to men's hearts. And still she walked, and still the sky rained, but now, in the night she stood, for she had come to the barn; because the barn is where horses go, when they come back from pasture in the fall, when they finish a day's work. In the morning it's where they have their first oats, in the evening where they're fed their last meal with the brushing of their coats. Like dogs who come home from a hundred miles away, Nellie had an unerring instinct that led her around the bay and to the great barn doors of home. She stood now, stamping her hooves, waiting, knowing someone would come and shove the three-story doors wide. She let out a long loud neigh that arced through the air, winged over the road and slipped into the upper window, where Stella awoke. And knew the horse had come home.

She did not bother to dress. In her nightgown, she threw her covers back, and raced down the stairs barefoot. Through lightning flashing, crossing the road, the widening puddles and the rain that stung her shoulders like ice picks, she shoved the barn doors wide. Braided into the horse's mane were the first early shoots of a fern and a purple and green Jack in the Pulpit from the forest.

Inside lay David, soaked, asleep on the horse's broad back.

"Where?!" his mother shouted.

"Here. I brought him into bed. He's upstairs."

They peeked through the bedroom door.

Stella crossed the room and sat beside him on the bed, touched his hair. Held his hand in her own and brushed the hair from his face that had grown long and wild.

David sat up and rubbed his eyes.

"Sleepy," he said.

"Yes."

"'Fraid, Stella."

"No more 'fraid now, David."

"No more," David said.

"You stupid idiot! We send you across the bay for wood

and you don't come back for . . four months?? What did you think you were doing disappearing?!"

"Hush, Mother! He's just come home."

"I *won't* hush! We send him on a simple task for lumber and he takes off??"

"I have lumber, Mama."

"You don't have lumber. Stop lying."

"Yes, I do."

He rose and walked downstairs, *clump-clump.* And opened the door, *squeak,* and walked across the porch, *creak,* and down the porch steps, *thump,* and across the dirt road, *crunch,* and up to the barn, where the rain graced his face light as feathers.

"Grace," he said, for that was his mother's name, and until then he had never spoken it. She stopped suddenly, looked at him, opened her mouth, and closed it as he pushed the barn doors wide.

Inside, Nellie stood chewing hay. Beside her lay sixteen eight by fours of lumber to reside the holes the raccoons made in the maple syrup shack. Plus forty crates for the potato crop.

"Where did you get all this?!" She raised her hand as if to slap him.

"Mama, your name is Grace, but the Quaker told me that you don't act like grace. He said that if your name is Grace you'd better learn how to *act* like it."

"You made that up!" she said. And she spun on her heel, but before she strode through the barn doors and out, back to the house, the foreman blocked her path.

"Who are you?! What are you doing in my barn?" she shouted.

"When the horse pulled off and came to this barn as we were passing, I realized this must be the boy's house. I have heard from the boy of his life in your house, and I will tell ye clearly, so that ye understand exactly what I'm saying, so that I don't have to come back and tell ye twice. Ye will no longer yell at this boy, not once. Ye will treat him like the man he has proven himself to be. If at any time, I hear that ye have beat him, hurt him, yelled at him, or in any way impinged one bad word on his soul, I will hunt ye down, I will tie yer arms to the largest oak in the forest, and I will leave ye there to die. Do I make myself clear to ye? Ma'am?"

Her lips parted, her eyes flashed, and then she closed them.

"Good. David, son, here is yer pay. Men! Let's move on."

"Did you do what I told you?" Stella brushed his arm and took his hand beside the bed, where he was happily and sleepily ensconced in clean jammies after the departure of the men.

"Yes, I did," he said.

"I knew you would."

"You owe me chocolate cake, Stella."

"I owe you *chocolate* cake?"

"You do."

"You think I should make it right now?"

"You better."

"You going to yell at me for not making it before you got here?"

"I'm not yelling, Stella."

"It sounds like you are."

"Look, Stella."

"Where?"

"There."

Through the window, the wolves sat on the ridge, looking east over the bay, and as the sun raised its head out of the cradle of the horizon, they lifted their voices, singing and singing, calling the silent ones home.

---

# THE RELIGION
# OF LOSS

S pring sunlight trembled slenderly down the sides of rough trunks. Scratching in the underbrush. What... "Quick! Get your pail!" Along the scant deer trail my mother's urgent voice sped.

"But you can't put light in a pail!" I was six years old, running after.

In wet spring leaves at a maple's base, she brushed unruly hair behind her ears, scuffed at the moist mat of last autumn's leaf fall, startled and pointed. A thin beam of sun graced a faded cross leaning into old bark where an Ojibwa man died, poisoned by his lover for loving Morel mushrooms more than her. They poked up from his body, curled and succulent to the tongue, o-da-naw-naw, brown buttery, paw-tay-son, soft as plums in my mother's hand. From death to live, this is what she told me:

"The Morel mushroom looks like it has a brain which doesn't attach to its head."

I clapped my hands to my head to see if my brain were attached.

"But the poisonous mushroom, its brain cap does

attach to its head. See? Ack! Poisonous." She mock-frowned, squatted, dug a hole in the rich damp earth, dropped the bad mushroom in, stood up, tamped the soil with her toe.

Scratching with fingernails in the clumped earth, I quickly dug it out, trembling, fearful. Peering around, I saw she had disappeared. I jumped up, crying shrilly, stumbling on the path, unable to see her shape through the trees. If she didn't want my brain attached to my head, I didn't know how to get it off.

Sometimes when I'm remembering, I hear her say, very clearly, my Ojibwa father's name when she buried the poisonous mushroom. I have an extraordinary ear for musical sound. I remember the tenor and tone, the cant and rhythm of my mother's voice. But I have no ear for actual words and have to refill her tones to cover for those words about my father that passed out of memory the moment they were spoken and placed me at her peril instead. So it could be, everything I say is a lie, but if it is, it's born from a gift and an unknowing.

It is not intentional. And you must forgive me. I was only six at the time.

◆

Halting so quickly, I smacked into the seat of her pants, pressing my fingers on her clothes. This was an action that as a child I did often, touching to make sure the parent was still where she said she was.

Hovering like horseflies, we teetered blinking on the high hill of a sunny meadow. Bees rang out in rich harmony, grasshoppers sang "whir-click-ee!" A measureless wind lay the long grass down so flat, the steeple of the Presbyterian Church below the slope appeared and disappeared with each sharp gust. Bells rang out with perilous intent, and chimed shut.

My mother lifted her head, sniffed the afternoon air. One hair loosened, curled and tendrilled. Like a mare spring-loosed to pasture, she lifted one skinny leg up, tossed both arms over her head and danced out into the sun. She bounded her long thin legs high above the tall grass, while round her head that wild red mane flung itself free. A frolicking baby colt, I hopped out after, loose-limbed and splay-legged, until she dropped into a low squat and lay flat as if to sun herself, yanking me down so quickly, I fell face-first into the dirt.

Out of the path through the woods a man came limping, shifting from his bad leg to his good, so that the effect was that of a shuffle-run. He was tall, taller than my mother who seemed as tall as the sky to me, and slender as he was tall. I recognized the white collar, the long nose, the hogshead chest, the lidded eyes of the Reverend Peter Tandoor. As it flapped down the aisle to the pulpit every Sunday, the sole of his shoe flapped now with a sad slap-slap against the earth.

My mother did not spring up as he tramped past, though we were going the same way. And he merely glanced at us, his eyes wandering over my mother, and went on across the meadow, seeds of grass trailing from him in the heated, lingering air.

My mother sat up, sucked a passing seed from his coat onto her tongue, and swallowed it whole. Resting her finger to her lips with a smile and taking my hand, she set off after him in the same kind of limping shuffle as he.

Down onto flat ground, he crossed the gravel road in front of the church, stepped up onto a stone step and up again. He trod quickly the sagging gray porch boards of the parsonage and let slam the screen door behind.

We leapt down the embankment, but instead of turning

toward the parsonage, we spun round, crossed the road and entered the church.

The heavy wooden door swung in with effort, an old door scraping against the dull wood floor.

Dust floated dimly in gray light from the high narrow windows. A sullen red carpet tramped meanly from door to altar. The organ sulked hulking in its corner. The shadowy empty pews held eyes beneath.

My mother's breath leapt rapid behind me, frantic.

A shadow closed a door in the corner; I shied back. Impatiently, she shoved me forward her hand on my head insistent.

Would she hold me to her?

But no, my mother sat me in a pew in the rear, slipped her hand from mine, pinched one crayon between my two fingers, and tugged a church bulletin from the rack. This she laid, with a small wooden flute from her pockets, on the pew. She cautioned me in strict tones not to move and touched her lips to my forehead. The door creased the floor behind her, rasping shut.

Locked into position, my knees drawn up beneath my chin, my arms clasped tightly around my knees, I dared not stir. I knew if I did my mother would never come back. This was simple logic to me, one thing certain upon the other. If I moved, God would pass his hand over me and hide me from the one person I loved most.

And I fell quickly into an odd sleep, overwhelmed by an exhaustion I could not name.

Between eyelids, dim light from the high windows shimmered dustily, thinned, and vanished into night.

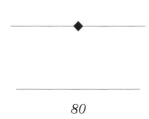

I awoke to nightmare clamoring. It was not an echo; it did not exactly repeat itself. It rang, skipped a measure and rang again.

I placed a hand over my heart. My heart was pounding! But no. The sound was this: a THUMP, and a clanging echo. THUMP-clang, THUMP-clang. Whoever heard of a heart resounding THUMP-clang, THUMP-clang? How small the world becomes in fear! Just me, and my heart! THUMP-clang! Those two drawn-out syllables were rhythmic, coming regularly, one after the other, until I realized, because I understood sounds far better than visions or smells or tastes or words, that it was the same pealing out I heard distantly from home. More distinctly it rang here, a slow, lonely, ringing out from high above. And then silence.

I did not know who rang, or what they rang for.

◆

Sundays, my mother force-marched me to services in this church. We always sat up front in the first pew while behind us people rustled their bulletins. Before us an enormous stained- glass window climbed from floor to ceiling and lit up the pulpit with harsh sunlight.

Precisely at noon, the Reverend Peter Tandoor stepped up to the brightly lit pulpit and that brightly colored light from the window caught him on fire. I do not lie. His long nose seared into flames, his robes blazed at the seams, the outline of his body scorched and burnt at his fraying edges. Maybe if he'd been more monster-sized than he was, he would have burnt more slowly. As it was, fire banished his words and I heard nothing of what he said. I merely trembled in God-given fear, because wasn't it God who talked through the burning bush; God now talking through the burning minister?

I was not a child who understood words. "Leper!" he roared, and "resurrection!" he bellowed, and "the blood of the body!" he howled. No one had to tell me why he yelled: he was a furnace.

Would he re-appear from the fire drenched in blood, white-scaled like a leper, his palms nailed to the cross on the window prior to resurrection? I prayed for mercy, begged God in my heart not to set fire to me. I didn't want to die in flames.

My mother, on the other hand, sat rapt. I cringed and cried and clawed at her, until she pierced me with a look. I sobbed not-too-silently into my mother's arm. Surely he was dead and burnt, a charred critter who would step down to give the blessing and fall to ashes on the floor.

But then … out of the sun-drenched pulpit, the Reverend re-appeared — and he did this magic every Sunday — unsinged, unscarred, only slightly pinkish to accept the collecting of tithes during the benediction. He didn't look burnt to me.

I whispered my concern to my mother.

She linked her arm over my shoulders. "You do not need to see to believe," she patted my hair.

But I did not know what she meant.

◆

Now, in the silence, the church shrank towards me in its darkness. Despite growing shadows, up the steps beside the window, a tiny hanged man began to appear in my vision, tied to a small cross. So this was what was on the wall behind the pulpit on Sundays! I knew who he was; I wouldn't be fooled.

Drawn to the cross, I risked stepping shakily out of the pew, looking all the while back over my shoulder, thinking:

Mama? Did you slip in without my knowing and see if I was sitting where you left me? And leave again? But no, no; I guess not. You're not there.

Belief without vision, is that what she said; is this what she meant? That I should be able to be here without seeing her? Was that faith?

I tiptoed forward to the next pew, edged the flute out of my pocket, blew a few notes, ran the scales. When in doubt, I trusted the only thing I understood: a hollow stick with a line of holes and the wind running through it. Sliding into the front pew, I sank onto its creaking surface and the song filling my head I did not push away, but let come.

Light outside the high windows gathered up, released the last of its dim glow, lowered its wick, and tamped down into night.

I was ready. Music was a gift I knew I had, and I knew how to use it to calm myself. My mother had taught me many times.

I played the gentle pat-a-pat of warm rain on spring green leaves. I played fresh Morel mushrooms from a damp, fertile ground. I played a red-maned mare dancing crazy in a meadow. I played the silver-shiny backs of salmon swimming along the night through the rippled river. I played my father standing poised on the bank with a hundred other men holding pitch forks, stabbing by flashlight into the dark fertile moistness.

I could see him there. And then I could see him fight, but then I couldn't. I didn't know. Over what?

I took the flute from my mouth, wiped it off and stood looking around. My heart thumped fearfully. So I lifted the flute again.

I played quietness in the church, shadows growing long from the ceiling, the devil lurking in the dark corner where the back door closed when we came in. I rubbed my cold arms. It was a long way in mind from the meadow to here, and I don't know where that song came from. I didn't think the devil had horns.

I quick played the Reverend booming from the pulpit, as if the devil and he were with me now.

But that wasn't true. See, I understood this: God doesn't come when there's only one child calling.

I heard rustles at the door; I heard the door creak. Afraid it was not my mother, or worse: that it was, I sat down stiffly.

I would not turn.

She couldn't make me.

I wasn't going to show how much I missed her. I was so angry at her for leaving me, I wanted to sit in our pew and sulk until God came down from heaven and told her off. But my eyes started to water, my knees trembled with sudden relief. And in my weakness, I ran silently back alongside the shadowy pews, seeing the dust in the dimly lit air moving before me, hearing my own little feet pounding on the carpet.

And I threw myself into her arms.

"Aieee!" the thing hissed. It grabbed my hand. Yanking furiously, I tried to shake it off. Hoisting me up, it dragged me up the aisle. I fought and screamed and kicked. Squeezed under its biceps, I tried to bite its underarm.

This wasn't my mother! This was the Devil, yes it was! I moved, didn't I? I moved when she told me not to. Surely my mother loved me enough to come running if she heard. But she didn't. I thought all this time, she was just outside the door. Now I knew for a fact she wasn't anywhere at all.

Maybe, it was just the beginning of what was to come.

A filthy, torn scarf slipped sideways to show a few long white hairs over the large and bony head. A horrible hissing and wheezing whistled between crooked brown teeth. Reeking from torn clothes amidst caked blood and dirt was the rank scent of fish scales, the muddy riverbank, the calluses of a pitchfork red on its hands.

I had heard enough, growing up amidst an inseparable mix of Ojibwa and biblical stories, to know that children and goats were routinely sacrificed at the Presbyterian altar to satisfy an angry God. Surely this was God now! He'd slap my hand in the fire, snap my bones with his two brown teeth, torch my skin with his one red eye! I was going to die in fire. I believe, Mama, I believe!

But at the altar it abruptly turned left, let go of my arm and hurled me into the organ pit. I scuttled back on the bench, rubbing the red imprints where the fingers had gripped, shutting my eyes so tight I saw stars.

"What are you fighting me so hard for?"

Wha ... ?

The head bowed over the rim of the organ where it held itself up with one hand. The bones stood out, gaunt and sharp-given to corners, the skin of arms reddened with old and fresh welts. Under the ragged eyebrows one good eye blinked, pulling the face down. There seemed to be no place where that sad eye stopped; it sagged on down to his toes, where I thought if I looked his chin would be propped.

He sank into the metal folding chair which the organist used between services. Laying his arms along his thighs and hanging his wrists loosely over his knees, he dangled his hands in the air and lowered his head below his shoulders.

"Play for me," he whispered. "Anything."

My father.

He was only a few notes in my head, a short staccato phrase.

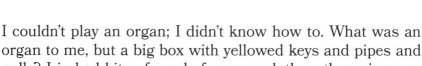

I couldn't play an organ; I didn't know how to. What was an organ to me, but a big box with yellowed keys and pipes and pulls? I jerked bits of candy from my clothes, the poisonous mushroom, fingerfuls of black dirt. Where was my flute?! His hands were dark on top, splattered with clinging fish scales, opalescent and hard.

"You dropped it," he nodded. I took it gingerly, careful not to touch him. "Play."

He knew my gift: that I could play what I could not express in words. But I . . ? Could I play ... what he ... ?

I followed the line of that grotesquely dirty and gnarled finger where an untended cut had festered green beneath the nail. From there my eyes leapt to the cross at which he pointed.

Some people say that a gift works in a child like a light bulb going on. But I heard it start distinctly as a small "ping." It was like a floodgate latch unsprung, with the rush of water tumbling out as both the memory and the music rush in.

I looked at the cross. Closing my eyes, I played what I knew. I heard it Sundays in the sermons, although I did not understand the theme of it in words. I knew only the feel of it, the pull and sense of it, the long high notes and the low, low deep "C." I played not my father's song, whatever it was, but the music that belonged to that man on the cross.

And I can't say I understood him either.

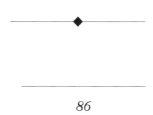

I played a child's birth with a doomed legacy, only the sound, the unspoken dark notes of minors and flats. I played a young boy with a voice from God: major C, sweet major G. I played a child who was not afraid to be alone: strong D and D diminished seventh wherein the fear trembled and then was taken up. I played a man who was listened to, because his words were carefully chosen, a tired man whose compassion was spoken: powerful F, soft E flat. I would have played the last supper, but I did not yet know what betrayal sounded like.

I did not know then how close my own loss was.

The music may have only been noise to my father, but it pealed out from the flute, circled up to the dark cross, wrapped itself around Christ's body, leapt across the stained glass window, turned and pealed out the open door, where I heard its distant moan and lilt echoing out across the night bay, where Te-bik-ke-zes, the Ojibwa moon, like God, was silent.

My father. Leaning forward, one finger lifted dank black bangs from my face. I scuttled away from him on the organ bench.

"Pe-sen-do-we-shin. Listen to me," he coughed black spittle onto the floor. His voice crackled hoarse and his face reddened, as if with fever. He lifted his head.

"Ke-gus-kaw-naw-baw-gwe naw?" I asked him if he wanted some water. My father leaned back in the chair and clasped his hands in between his knees and rocked the chair back. I brought him holy water, standing close to his knee, and looking in his face. Placing both hands on the silver bowl, he held the vessel up, and drank silently. Lowering it, he held it out again. I took it from him, replaced it on the altar, empty.

"I was not always like this," he rasped and spit black phlegm to the floor where it pooled. "It is not your mother's fault.

Ke-gaw-she," he sighed. "I don't know what she wants." He placed an unlaced wet boot over the phlegm.

My father bowed his head to this hands, then peered at me through his fingers, and took his hands from his face and closed them in his lap and leaned back and managed a slight smile.

"I'm sorry I scared you, little one."

"Papa? Where'd you come from?"

"Fishing for salmon."

"Fishing?"

"They're running up the Kenegun River to lay eggs."

"Oh. Did you get any?"

"Three big ones."

"How'd you know I was here?"

"I heard your flute."

"All the way over by the river?"

"All the way over by the river."

"You mean you could hear it that far?"

"I could hear you if I were on the other side of the world."

"Really?"

"Really."

"It's a very good flute. Mummy gave it to me."

"I know."

"I think she made it for me."

"I think she did."

"Why are you here? Mummy said she'd be back in just a minute."

"How long have you been here?"

"Oh-h-h, since it was light, I think."

"Since it was ... ? All night?!"

"Oh no, Daddy. Just a few minutes, I'm sure. I fell asleep because I was scared, but it wasn't ... long ... was it? She said she'd be right back."

"Do you want to come home with me?"

"I can't go. If I leave she won't come back."

"She tell you that?"

"She said or else."

He sighed a deep long rasping sigh that ended in a cough. He lowered his head into his hands and I saw his hands shake. But I didn't know why. I thought to pat his shoulder, and almost did, but then didn't. I was trembling like a little bird ruffling its wings in the cold.

"You come when you're ready. I'll wait for you at the door."

"No! Don't go! I don't want you to go! I don't want to be alone again!"

"I'm not going anywhere except to the door to wait for you."

"Why are you going to wait for me?"

"Because it's time to go."

"But Mummy won't know where I am."

"Mummy always knows where you are."

"She doesn't! She didn't come back and check on me when I was crying! She doesn't know anything! Mummy's bad!"

"Mummy's having a hard time right now. She needs to go away."

"Away? Where!"

"I don't know."

"Is she coming back?"

"Come on, it's time to go now."

"Will she be mad if I go?"

"No. She'd probably like it if you came home with me."

"She would?"

"Don't you think she wants you to be safe?"

"Yes, I think she does. She said that's why she brought me here. Can I just say goodbye to the church?"

"I'll wait for you by the door."

"Bye, Papa."

"I'll wait for you."

"Okay."

He walked to the window behind the pulpit where the fire did not burn, turned on his heel and strode out. I crept out of the organ pit and stood at the front of the church. Looking down the carpet, I watched my father's silhouette push the big old door wide. The rain had begun through the open door, and its spears flashed in the dark like crystal breaking, while wind blew leaves in along the carpet and beneath the pews. I smelled his river odor lingering and trailing to the door.

Turning to the man on the cross, I thought to say something. But I couldn't think what. And then I remembered, and put my hands together and kneeling below him on the carpet, said: " If she comes, tell her I've gone with my dad, so she won't worry." And I clambered down the one step to the rug. And turned and knelt again: "Amen." Charging down the aisle and outside, I moved the big door heavily to close it and was startled by the blackness of night. Beside me the figure of my father sank to the ground and cried.

Racking, heaving gasps ripped from him, river water dripped from him, pooled from his mouth and his eye and his nose. And when he rose slowly and wearily to his feet, he pointed. "I will wait for you right there next to that tree. Please go tell her I'm sorry." He dropped one large salmon at my feet and, hefting the two over his shoulder, he disappeared up the embankment. I could still see his large shape, standing under the limbs of a large maple, melding into the trunk, darker than shadows.

The rain jabbed me like ice picks, but I had been asked to do this, and I was still a good kid then. Wrapping the gill rope around both fists, I dragged the heavy fish by lunging and yanking and heaving it along the gravel road. It was as long as I was tall, and kept slapping the ground with its tail because it was not dead. Smack, smack, smack. Iridescent scales scraped off on small stones, and when I turned to look behind, the path gleamed luminescent in the rain.

In the silver drizzle, in the dark night, on the graveled road, the salmon finally was too much for me to pull. I dropped it before I reached the minister's porch and let it lay.

How did I know where my mother was? Perhaps I was drawn merely by the light; I do not know. In fact, I do not know that she was there at all.

I knocked twice. The Reverend answered, dressed in pants and a white shirt with the sleeves rolled up, tucking his shirt into his pants. I said, as any six-year-old would: "I want my mother."

But he did not reply. And she did not come. Instead, looking out at the road, he stepped out onto the porch, down the stone step and strode to the gravel road with the rain beating on him. Reaching down, he picked up the gill rope and he picked up the salmon whose tail slapped the ground a weak slap. He walked back with it in his arms, and stepping up onto the step, turned into the parsonage door and closed the door with the great fish in his arms, until only a thin light showed through the window, and even that seemed scant enough to see by.

Like rain sprung loose and falling, I shook, until remembering, I turned and made my way to the tree. My father picked me up and hugged me close, carried me all the way through the dark woods, over the moonlit meadow, along the slender path through the trees and back into my mother's house, where she no longer stepped.

And I lived with him there until the music my mother had taught me ceased to play in my head, and I learned that life with my father began with the sound of one fish slapping the dark wet fertile ground.

# WINGS TO FOLLOW

Octber. I confide to my sister, Eliza, I've been thinking about crossing the Mackinac Bridge into Canada on horseback.

"What's the matter with a car?"

"Don't have one."

"People going that way."

"I know it."

"If you insist on doing it the fool's way, you should know there's two bridges and fifty miles in between."

"Didn't know that."

"Ask anybody. One gets you onto the Upper Peninsula and the next one sets you off in Ontario. What for?" She is drying glasses with a dirty towel behind the bar in the Au-Ne-Pe Tavern in Kenegun. It is mid-afternoon, and the rain from the morning has turned back into snow and is turning again to rain. It is October in Michigan, less than a year since Papa died last January. The road is thick with grey snow and the cars going by look battered and smeared with grime and the road is starting to slush and run with melt because the snow is too early.

Eliza chokes and coughs and hacks, has to set the glass down on the bar and wipe her eyes with her sleeve.

"If I'd known you'd thought it was so funny, I would have brought a crowd."

She shakes her head, winks at me, picks up a full bar tray and skirts around the edge of the bar. From a smoky booth, a man's boot pokes out and trips her. The tray tips; a bottle wobbles and falls and splashes and rolls, sputtering beer on the stained floor. Eliza looks at the bottle, measures it and the man in the booth in the same hard glance, picks up the bottle by inserting her finger into the neck, and moves on.

"Hey! Where's my goddamn beer?"

She sets the bottles down on a small tray near the pool table and turns back toward the bar. I see the hand that set the pool cue down give her a shove, so that she drops the tray with the empties on it. I am half out of my chair, but she waves me down, picks the bottles up between her fingers, walks coolly behind the bar, all grim eyes and hard angles, and slams the tray down.

I see the gun under the counter, below the cash register. A small neat Browning automatic with a clip lying beside it. She snaps the clip into the gun, lays it on its side, loaded. Her face is guarded, hard and watchful. It's like she's got a sixth sense for trouble and that sixth sense switch is on all the time.

A hot light over the pool table dulls the rest of the bar into shadows. The young voice that cursed her has come from underneath. Voices murmur, rise, and fall from the dark booths.

"I know that voice, Eliza. I've seen him around school."

"Y'want your beer, you can come and get it." She looks straight at the boy, who walks over. He looks to be about my age, fifteen or so, stringy black hair to his chin, thin, childish face, jeans slipping below his hips in the latest middle school boys' style.

He reaches fast to snatch the beer from Eliza's hand, but she shows him her coyote teeth and holds on tight. He works to get it out of her grip, and she suddenly lets go. He falls back, but catches the bottle before it hits the floor, straightens up and stares at her.

"Y'got strong teeth to open it, d'you?" she asks, with the innocence of a bystander, and closes her coyote teeth behind her lips.

He hesitates, then hands it back to her, swings around on one boot heel and grins at his friends. She twists the beer cap off the bottle under the counter, pours the beer out across the bar until it fizzes and runs over the edge and down the front of his pants. He jumps back, surprised. She picks up the gun with one hand and points it at his crotch. Instinctively, he covers his crotch with his hand, and his surprise breaks the sneer on his face.

"Now you tell me," Eliza whispers up close to his ear but loud enough for me to hear, "since you piss me off. If you were me, would you think you was under age? You tell me. Would you load this fucking gun thinking maybe you were under age and about to make me lose my license serving beer to you?" The boy looks over at his friends. They stand quiet on the other side of the light, only their flannel shirts and their belts and the tops of their pants and their hands on the pool cues are visible between the hot overhead light and the green felt of the pool table. The boy backs away, looks again to them, a pleading look.

"Y'got your I.D.? Y'got nothing in your pants but a pickle teaser that's already getting you into trouble?"

She lays down the gun under the bar, and the boy drops his shoulders, stands with the look on his face alternating from uncertainty to defiance.

I always take it as a rule that you don't talk back to a

woman who's just held a gun on you, but this boy's got brains in his underwear.

"I got proof."

But Eliza doesn't answer, keeps her eyes steady on him, washes one glass, sets it upside down on a towel and washes the next. I know he was the one that pushed her. I saw the gold watch on his arm he probably mugged some weak old man for. He's just not smart enough to know his goose is cooked. I lean on the bar, take a sip from my Coke and enjoy the show. I watch him swagger toward his friends, but he stops before he gets there, rocks uncertainly back and forth like he can't decide whether to go forward or backward. If I were him I'd go sideways and shoot out right out the front door before Eliza does something he's going to be sorry for. I squint over at his friends, but see nothing because of the light except what's happening on the pool table. One shoots, banks the cue ball off the side rail.

"Ain't I eighteen? Hey! I'm talking to you. You tell her I'm eighteen like we was all agreed." They chalk their cue sticks, click them together side by side. The white ball hums in circles, banks off three rails. Cigarette smoke obscures the face, but the stick leans back and shoots forward and lifts up. Balls clink rapidly, rhythmically, cue ball into the ten, ten off the far rail into the eight, eight rolling near the pocket, landing tottering on the rim. From a dim booth in the back, somebody laughs.

The boy hitches up his pants and looks at Eliza and back over at his buddies. Then I see it, pointed and cruel but puny, a knife no better than for camping with the Boy Scouts, a tiny flint compared to the bear hunting knives I've seen men flash in here. I let out a low whistle, Eliza's and my signal since we were little kids running from our Papa. The tavern buzzes to a stop; heads in the booths peer out. Eliza holds her hands quiet in the soapy water, narrows her eyes on the boy, and her face grows cold and hard as a Petoskey stone rising out of the bay.

He glances back and forth, shuffles his feet, as if he is unsure, his pride all bent out of shape. Eliza gazes over her right shoulder toward the back of the bar where only the red Miller sign flicks on, flicks off, a red lighthouse in a sea of grey smoke.

"Hey, Harry!" She slips the towel off her shoulder, dries a glass, sets it rim down, picks up another, dries it round, sets it rim down, one at a time. "You got one here thinks he's big enough to play mumblety peg with a Barlow knife."

A large man of black and Indian mix appears out of a dark booth in the back, takes hold, one hand on the boy's belt and the other on his wrist, snaps the wrist and arm back until tears run out of the boy's eyes and the knife falls to the floor. I see from the fury in the boy's face he isn't going to say a word, but then Harry throws the boy into the street, and stoops down, picks up the switchblade from the floor and tosses it out between two parked cars as if it and the boy together were no more than dust to air. And the boy is cursing him now, standing there outside the door with the icy rain dripping on him, and the grey snow mucking around his feet, cursing worse now as if the devil had flown into his mouth and taken up residence there.

The tavern returns to its low buzz and hum.

Eliza grins across the bar at me, jerks her head at the street. "Potential boyfriend for you." I lay my hand on my heart. She takes the glass off the bar, places it rim side down on a toweled tray, picks up another, polishes it around the outside leaving the permanent spots and sets it upside down next to the last one. She is rhythm, my sister, her life measured out in knives and bar glasses and a Browning automatic. She throws the grimy towel over one hard shoulder, sets her two reddened hands on her thin hips, leans over and looks at me.

"What."

She waves her arm mockingly at the dingy walls and beer and blood-stained carpet and the Miller sign on the wall flashing on and off and at the one grey window to the street where last year's Christmas lights flicker dimly under their blanket of dust and to the three men, or are they boys, shooting the eight ball aimlessly back and forth. She comes out from behind the bar and puts her arm around me and turns me and stands me up like a doll so the few day-long patrons sitting on stools at the bar can look me over.

"Just look what we got here, folks. The first little Indian Calamity Jane. What you all think? Ain't she cute?" They all nod, remark, when she tells them, how they knew someone or other what took a horse across the Mackinaw Bridge once. Hell, they even knew someone who'd swum the dang horse across and nearly drowned.

"Au-tay yo-ko-kee. Swamp water they call that piece of sea," the old man Ta-kuh-mo-say sits at the bar, his back humped and unable to straighten up. "Old story has it that the Bearwalkers used to rise up out of there looking like fish and roll in the sand and dirt 'til they had their fur on right and proper. What come out of their mouths was nothing more than fire lit by natural gas rising up from the bottom of the bay and lighting the swamp peat they had slimed all over their tongues. Bearwalkers all right. You ask anybody they'll tell you." And he takes a swig of beer from his glass by putting his mouth down to the rim and tipping the glass forward, his old hands shaking with age.

I look in Eliza's face which is all hard and alert. I stand up and lean over and put my arms around her like I am going right now, and for all I know maybe I am, because I feel the distance rise up between us, and I take a step back and drop my arms again.

"What are you going for?" Eliza asks softly. She pours Jack Daniels and soda into a glass and slides it down the bar. We both watch it go.

"It's like the wind has started up inside me, Eliza, swirling like a cloud of white wet snow that won't let up until I ride out of here. Every afternoon I come down here after school and every afternoon I think about leaving. Something is different though for saying it out loud. Now it seems like I've got to live up to my word."

"What are ya really going for?" Eliza asks again, softly.

I lean forward and whisper: "Remember how we used to talk about where Mama was from?"

"Yeah, sure. Up around the Manitoulin Reserve. So?"

"Well, I'd just like to go see, that's all."

"You think she might be there?"

"I don't know. I think I'd like to find some people that are our kin."

"Well, you ain't got much to lose here." And she grins both a mischievous and sad grin at me. "Wish I could go," she says.

"Why don't you, Eliza? We could go together. Just think of it. We wouldn't have any money, and we don't have any horses, but we'd find some. Somebody who'd feel sorry for us walking all that way and give us a couple of strays. Why don't you do it, Eliza?"

Harry comes up behind her and empties out the cash register. He touches Eliza on the shoulder, and she turns, nods, smiles and turns back to me.

"I can't go," she says simply and commences polishing the bar with her grimy towel.

"Why not?" I feel the disappointment rising up hard, as if for a moment I thought we could.

"This is all I got. And sister?" She peers up into my face like a demented chipmunk until I laugh and put my hand on her face and push her away. "Somebody's got to be here for you when you come back to visit. Ain't no good coming back to your home when there's nobody here to welcome you."

"I didn't know you thought of this bar as our home."

"Best home I ever had," she says. "It pays me a living, supplies your overeager appetite with food and, *hell*, you got a bed to sleep in. What are you complaining for?"

"Pickled eggs. I'm going to throw up. And some bed. Harry gets it during the day, and I have to wait until he gets up."

"He works hard, Harry does."

"You drink too hard. You get beat up. There's better things, Eliza. This isn't worth it."

"No," she says. "You're right. It ain't. Come get me when you're rich and I'll pack my bags and we'll go make a Indian picture out in Hollywood."

Eliza walks me to the door and stands inside while I go out. Then she reaches through the door, holds it open with one hand, and hands me the Browning automatic and an extra clip. "Well, if you're going, take this. If you ain't, give it back."

"Didn't say I was going right now. I'm thinking about it."

"Shoot while you're thinking so you'll know how." She closes the door and goes inside. I zip my worn and torn Army/Navy coat she lifted for me from the coat rack. She comes back out, leans against the door in a short sleeve T-shirt, a cigarette dangling from her mouth, all hard angles and skinny bones. It is snowing fairly hard and the snow lands on her bare arms and sweeps in through the open door by her boots. "I hope you're taking Grandmother with you."

"To hell I will."

"Well then. Go get her and drop her off at the tavern on

your way. We'll let her hang out in the front window and scare people off."

I pass the boy crouched beneath a window of the diner, closed for the season, his knife clenched open in his hand and head bent against the sleet, waiting for his traitor friends.

I pass the old man, Ta-kuh-mo-say, sitting on a kitchen chair on the street corner, white flakes piling up on his ear-muffed hat, and the dirty water and the snow running under the chair's legs, over the curb and into the gutter where it flows unimpeded down toward the reservation.

"The Manitoulin reserve," the old man Ta-kuh-mo-say says. "That's where your mother comes from, where her people still are. Go north," he says, and points straight up, pulls loose tobacco from a pouch and tosses it into the air.

As if he thought I had wings to follow.

# HOW THE MORMON WIVES STOLE THE GOLD FROM DANIEL BEN LONG, KING OF THE MORMONS

Through November, the sky had the grey paunch so common among the northern islands, forebodingly heavy with winter. Daniel Ben Long climbed aboard the *Queen of the Great Lakes* to attend the legislature downstate.

Six times the steamship thrust full throttle before the expanding ice round the dock let it go. He held to his chest the documents of his Mormon faith and leaned over the railing to wave to his wives. But they had turned from the squalling wind, lifting their maroon shawls to cover their faces, and scurried along the dock to the shore. He thought he saw a snowball go back and forth between one or another.

But there's no indication here why he might have thought that.

By January, snow squalls crossed the ice of Lake Michigan in zigzag bursts, slamming against the women's cabin with a whomp! The one-room cabin lifted in the wind, leaned out over the ice, whistled back down. At night, for warmth, 17-year-old Samantha shared a bed with two of Elecmantha and Marguerite's six children and Melissa Alyssa Victoria.

With soft wispy hair, delicate voice and fragile skin, Melissa Alyssa smelled of daisies entwined in lilacs. Left by her father and brothers on board the *Queen of the Lakes* in contract marriage to Long, Melissa was a teacher. Not six months wedded to him, she was eighteen years old when he married Samantha. Melissa became, not the first wife with timeworn devotion, nor the second with the passion and punishment of Eve, nor even the fourth newest untempered and curious artist expected in time to heel to. In body and voice, she paled to a hollow shell and became ... nothing.

At night, one of Elecmantha's children cradled against her arm, Samantha whispered her belated instructions: "You should have fought like a wolverine and locked yourself in the ship's head like I did."

But Melissa just lay on her back and with the slenderest sense of humor replied: "It didn't seem to work for you," she smiled. "In my mind," she glanced up at the ceiling, "I'm in a convent with many kind nuns and God is my only husband."

"Why didn't you get off the boat?"

But Melissa just turned over and touched Samantha's red curls in the dark, saying quietly, "God doesn't pay dowry."

In the silent opening of February, Marguerite and Elecmantha hauled out the last twenty-pound bag of flour. Dragging it inside, they leaned it against the wall and, together, banged open the back door, strode out and popped the lid off a barrel. A raccoon's foot marks were visible on the last thin layer of molasses. "We'll starve," Elecmantha raised her large hands over her head and moaned. Golden hair fell in thin dry strands down her back.

Marguerite, who in figure and voice resembled a tiny cuckoo bird, pulled her russet shawl up against the wind, then paused and pointed across to the next hill.

"See that strange man walking above the tree line?"

"He's a hermit, I guess. Harmless, I'm sure."

"Harmless to whom?"

"I don't know."

"Is that a wolf following him?"

"I don't know that either."

"You don't know a lot, Elecmantha."

"I thought we were the only ones here."

Marguerite trudged back inside. "We'll have to send someone across the ice to Leelanau to ship supplies back by horse and sled. It'll be April before the regular boat can get back."

The ice sparkled on the lake.

"So who ... "

Marguerite pointed to Melissa.

"Not Samantha?"

"She's strong. We need her."

Inside, Melissa walked quietly to the front door and flung it open. The air stood frigid as a sentinel, too cold to breathe. From the dock below the hill out into the spectral distance, the ice twinkled and beckoned, but on the gaunt arm of a black branch in front of her, resplendent yellow, a chickadee cocked its head sideways from under its dark cap. Melissa held out her hand; the drop of an icicle plopped into it. Snow fell from the roof with a *whumph*. Early February, and the whole world seemed to be melting.

Melissa took a chair from the wall. She placed it next to Marguerite and Elecmantha who picked up their darning needles and spoke quietly, intensely and for a long time. At the hearth, at the word "Leelanau," Samantha looked up from her reading to the children and frowned.

Marguerite and Elecmantha glanced at Melissa then down at the table. Thumbing their fingers into the grooves where the wood had cracked, each felt in the stab of a splinter the sore pains of recent childbirth. A faint throb of shame rose in their minds that the weakest of them should do this. Who knew how far across the ice she would have to go? Newcomers, they didn't know how far. But Melissa insisted, as if she knew this to be her calling. As if there can BE a true calling.

Her fragrant breath grown thin as frost on Samantha's cheek, she lowered her eyes from Samantha's questioning eyes.

"Why *can't* I go with you?!" Samantha spoke hotly. She cast an odious look at Elecmantha and Marguerite, then flung herself into a corner by the wood box. The children, startled, leapt up and wrapped themselves around her.

Melissa rose. She was eighteen years old, delicate in bone, thin in face, yet a determination had thrown itself onto her slight frame. Feverish to the touch, anxious to get on, she pulled the string tight through the button hole of one of their husband's old coats, took a long harsh breath and walked out into the pale morning sun.

Stuffing dried venison into their lovely sister's pockets, Marguerite and Elecmantha trundled to the dock with Melissa, hugged her and prayed for her.

And let her go.

The cabin door banged open. Marguerite turned from Melissa and looked back as Samantha tore down the steep path, leapt from the dock with no coat on, and skidded out onto the ice, halted in her slide only by Melissa's outstretched arm. The wind came up as if to greet them.

She pulled Melissa's socked hand up, placed in it one blue-tipped feather of a heron, a piece of purple yarn wrapped around a pebble, a red bead no larger than a raspberry, and a long pale strip of green milkweed with the feathered seeds intact.

"I love you, Melissa Alyssa." They kissed, on the lips, and didn't care what the others thought. "So, what are you waiting for?" But Melissa just stared at her. Samantha shrieked: "Go!"

"You quit looking at me," Melissa lowered her eyes. Samantha slammed back up the hill. Marguerite and Elecmantha gazed stunned after her.

Later, Marguerite pushed the heavy door shut against the wind and, pulling off her scarf, glanced around to get a sense of the fire; did it need banking? But the large smoky room held blankets strewn with dirty boot prints; the precious fire trashed with melted snow; black ashes that streaked across the walls. Marguerite barked her little yippy dog bark then set to howling. Elecmantha gusted in behind her, stamping off snow. The large woman stood stunned, then, walked briskly over to Samantha, grasped her arm, pulled her onto her lap, and rocked my mother until night came on dark, and my mother's tears washed Elecmantha's skin, until Elecmantha's hard red psoriasis grew pink and soft and shimmery-clean.

◆

In their journal, its frail leaves lying open before me now, I see the two older women penned these words cryptically into the margins of Long's Bible, taking turns in the handwriting to get the words to curl around the corners of the page. "We saw her stare south, shading her eyes. The sunlight glinted on the ice, making it hard for us to see. Maybe she could see the twenty miles to Leelanau before she arrived. Her young sight must be better than ours."

But I have been out on the ice on a clear day. And I have stood where my mother's friend stood, and could not see Leelanau Peninsula, and have been told by others living on Beaver Island now, that you cannot see Leelanau from Beaver.

It's too far.

◆

Late February, west of Beaver Island, the wide eye of a blizzard exploded eastward across the ice, its snow squalls rupturing north to south.

O-da me-tchaw-ne's head snapped up on his scrawny neck, a hairless white cannonball rising on a string. He scanned the breadth of the storm, estimating its speed. At his feet, two black bass slapped the ice, a rainbow trout banged its body defiantly up and down, and a small perch lay still. He tugged the dropline until the hook popped up through the ice fishing hole, then coiled the line and laid it in his creel.

Red, white and blue remnants of gill net and rusty fish hooks were embedded so deep into his beard, he thought a woman would prick her fingers if she tried to stroke it. Clumsily, he sawed with a flint knife to cut two new hooks out, wondering why a woman had not yet wanted to *touch* his beard. Maybe it was the color. He could dye it with plant tinctures. This was a vain thought for a man half-Jesuit, half-Ottawa Indian.

A few feet away, a wolf lay on the ice, her head up, sniffing the air. The wind ruffled her fur. "Mabel," he whispered. "You like it this way? Also this way?" Her ears pricked forward.

With startling quickness, the first wind squall unfurled its baggage. The onslaught of snow knocked him back and he bent his head into it.

O-da me-tchaw-ne jammed the gill rope with two salmon to his belt hastily. He shoved open the top to his creel and dropped in the trout and the perch. Banging the lid shut, he slung the creel and his burlap pack over his shoulders. Striding with ear flaps wide and tugging in the wind, he steered toward Beaver Island and his tiny cabin on the eastern shore. At a half-run, his curved back, splitting with streaks of pain, bent into the gale. His beaver-lined boots left no track as the wind swept all life signs away.

Mabel's surly wolf's head rose and followed, nose to heel.

He strode fast now, head down, not daring to turn around on the ice. A man could get lost in this blizzard, panic dragging him in God-knows-what-direction, until he fell foolishly into his own darn fishing hole. Didn't he know Joe Hollis had misstepped year before last, one blackened, frozen glove stuck fingers up to the inside edge of his ice fishing hole? That hole Oda me-tchaw-ne had come upon in the wake of a snowstorm, the thin skim of fresh ice still on it. As if Joe Hollis had tried to climb out, and changed his mind. As if God didn't just reach up when you were not looking and yank you under.

Shrieking, the snow pounded him, whiteness blinding him. He paused, waited. Waited, feeling the wolf waiting behind him. Mabel nudged his knee. The curtain parted briefly. Boulders at the shore's edge were within a quick run. He allowed himself one glance at the Mormon women's cabin on the hill, which he used as a marker, knowing his own house squatted on the shore below. He turned, stepped sharply, stumbled and fell.

Surprised at his clumsiness, he hoisted himself onto one knee, boosted himself up with the wolf whining and nosing him, but tripped again, slipped on the ice and skidded. Mabel howled. The two errant gilled ones flopped away across the ice. The wolf charged after them, snapping at their gills, her toe nails scratching across the rough surface. His right knee felt half torn off while his face, numbed on the rough surface, smacked up against a woman's fragile features frozen stone-cold solid to the ice.

He sang out sharp, scrambling back now, howling more like a wolf than a man, but with a richness of timbre that Mabel could never achieve. The wolf crept forward, sniffed, licked the woman's face. This, O-da me-tchaw-ne knew, was a prelude to Mabel's determining the edibility of the woman's flesh. He wrenched the wolf's hind feet out from under her, and Mabel's hard jaw banged down on the woman's cheek.

Pale as the ice itself, the woman's skin broke in fine lines. A first layer crumbled like opals, skittering across the ice. Her eyes blue and distant gazed at him with a look he translated first to pity, secondly to love. He knew without knowing she had been in love with someone when she died, and he felt that love now in his own marrow, in his own big heart, as if it had been he.

Yes, he said. Even *I* could have been loved.

Never daring to approach when she was alive, it was doubtful she had ever seen his shy presence. But he had glanced at her among the trees, across the hills, and come to know certain things about her. The two older women shouting at her. The way she danced alone amidst the young maples, sashaying round a sapling, singing softly. Often he had seen the young red-haired beauty that walked at her side among the trails, giving her a hug now and again.

Her lips had turned black, but to him they still seemed red. So had her fingernails, though to him they were soft pink. Held to her face, her hands had frozen with a gesture so delicate, he thought he would cry with the beauty of them.

No newcomer to snow squalls, he tore himself from that

lovely face, scrambled up, chased after the flopping lake trout, caught and smacked them a good one with his fists. Pounding their sides until they were dead, he kicked them solidly, thumping and thumping until their scales scattered in the wind, then retied them, knotted, on his belt with just barely enough time to retrace his steps before the storm blotted out his new lovely vision forever.

He kissed the air next to her lips, so as not to offend her, and offered his thanks to a Lord God far mightier now than he had ever imagined.

She was the first woman he had seen close up in fifteen years.

For reasons no one in northern Michigan could figure or even the scientists who study the eccentric meteorological perversions of the great lakes, Lake Michigan, with its usual bent toward mysteriousness, thawed. In the middle of February, in the coldest winter on record, it thawed. During this thaw, which lasted less than twenty-four hours, and before the lake's grey surface froze solidly again, O-da me-tchaw-ne chipped the woman out of the ice.

The ribs of fools and freighters were visible near the surface where O-da me-tchaw-ne roped his lumber boat to the only dock on Beaver Island and brought Melissa Alyssa Victoria Long home.

The United States Postal Office on the Leelanau Peninsula commissioned the *Queen of the Lakes* to deliver the mail to the islands whenever there occurred a thaw. The captain, familiar with the great lakes' eccentricities for de-icing and re-icing, spewed a white canvas bag, a whole side of beef, and Daniel Ben Long out onto the Beaver Island dock, and steamed away through thick ice floats that threatened to lock the boat in.

O-da me-tchaw-ne had just managed to scuffle his frozen burden out of his lumber boat and tip her up onto the dock's planking. He paused, his acute hearing listening to the boat's arrival. When it ground against the dock, spraying cold water over him, his back seized up. Painfully, he glanced sideways.

The tall thin severe man fit the rumors the hermit had heard about Daniel Ben Long. He knew too, with the kind of sixth sense hermits have about other folk, that if this furious fellow *were* Long, the chap might have a dangerously wrong idea about what O-da me-tchaw-ne might be doing with his wife. Daniel Ben Long, he had heard, was very proprietary.

To the Ottawa, O-da me-tchaw-ne meant He-Has-A-Big-Heart. But O-da me-tchaw-ne's heart was not big toward human beings. O-da me-tchaw-ne was the kind of man who needed quiet, extended pauses, one sentence spoken with a long wait before the next. With their impatient eyes and tapping fingers, people hurried his thoughts, confused him as to what he had been thinking, until he felt moved to do what he had not intended.

On his father's Jesuit side, he was a decent, extremely though erratically religious man. On his mother's Ottawa side, he had a distrust and a sixth sense for people as well as a slight common sense. This brought him enough words to get by. And so he used what sense he had now, to find words that might protect him from death. And although he chose an obvious lie, the religion he chose was not unnoticed by Long.

"I am a Mormon." And he sunk his head to his chest.

Daniel Ben Long said nothing, but his entire posture suggested an enormous rage.

O-da me-tchaw-ne, not realizing rage was Long's normal posture, carefully, gently, set down on the dock the end of the frozen block that was Melissa, Long's wife. Instead of stepping backwards into his boat as he thought he should have if he were wiser, O-da me-tchaw-ne glanced down at the lovely face of his love. His heart gave a groan and he stood his ground, or, since his back wouldn't let him straighten up, stood his ground bent over.

The snow, which had paused briefly, fell once more on the men's shoulders, while the wind lifted their coat ends and pocket flaps, and laced and ruffled their beards as if it could act as intermediary.

Long, eyeing O-da me-tchaw-ne, slipped his hand into his coat pocket and flicked out a Bowie knife, the size of a cutter for bear skin.

O-da me-tchaw-ne moved quickly.

Scrambling down the bank to the shore, he knew death required choices one must not leave to chance. If I drown, he thought, maybe they will bury me near my love. If he knifes me, he will throw me in the lake. But then, a contrary thought came. What if the Mormons don't bury people at all? What if they put them in trees like his mother's ancestors? And so he hesitated before throwing himself in.

Aiming with a furious eye, the thin, severe man lifted his knife high and stabbed down hard. The blade chipped off a tiny nick of Melissa's ice block, skidded away on the dock, slipped between the planks and splashed into the depths below. Enraged, he fell on the block of ice, scraping it with his fingernails, chomping at it with his teeth, but the serene Melissa remained oblivious to her husband's torment. As he lay breathing hard on the block of ice, Long seemed to become aware of O-da me-tchaw-ne, standing at the end of the dock.

Leaping up, he grabbed O-da me-tchaw-ne, laced his arms around the large man's chest, doubled him backwards, wrenched him to the right, wrenched him to the left, and with a resounding pop-pop, O-da me-tchaw-ne stood up straighter than he could ever remember.

Wheezing, Long backed up onto the rocks. But before O-da me-tchaw-ne could thank him for the adjustment that he felt deeply, the Mormon hefted one side of the block that was Melissa and, nodding to the Jesuit to lift the other, rose to one knee. O-da me-tchaw-ne, a man suddenly released from years of stultifying back problems, grinned. If he had not been weighed down by the block of ice, and the enraged man at the other end, the half-Jesuit, half-Ottawa bear of a man would have floated up the hill.

For the approximately twenty minutes it took the men to get Melissa up the snowy hill toward the cabin, a strange peace settled over Beaver Island. Even the birds began to chirp, as if spring had come.

◆

Hiding around the bend, the Michigan Tax Revenue boat pulled up to the dock at the exact moment that Samantha — her shawl flung from her shoulders, her lungs heaving in anger — beat the tar out of her husband. And standing with his arms trembling at his sides, Long let her. Melissa's death was likely their only compassionate moment, if compassionate be the word where a wife hits her husband in the chest with a snowball with rocks embedded in it.

O-da me-tchaw-ne wisely removed himself to a tree.

Samantha stamped off west of the cabin. She did not detect O-da me-tchaw-ne in the tree beside her. Perhaps grief had wound itself around her too tight for her to see clearly. What she observed instead was a little man in a grey coat climbing out of a boat with "Michigan Tax Revenue" painted on its side. Hands on hips, shawl bound tightly around her head, Marguerite stood in front of this man at the dock, gesticulating, her words inaudible.

The cabin door slammed open. Frightened, O-da me-tchaw-ne flung himself from the tree down the steep hill behind the cabin. With head hanging from the beating he had just received, Long turned just in time to notice the tax boat at the shore, the little grey man climbing up the snowy hill, and his first wife gesticulating violently. He instantly launched himself at O-da me-tchaw-ne's deer hide heels. But Long's legs tangled on the icy slope and he banged into O-da me-tchaw-ne and sat down. Thus began their strange ride together down the icy hill, for a short intense period of their lives, with O-da me-tchaw-ne's legs splayed out in front, Long snugged up behind. Over snow-hidden rocks, with arms flung out, they careened into a big maple and bounced off to the side to lie heaped up in the deep snow.

Recovering from the sudden flight of the two men, Samantha watched as the two spoke words, then dug furiously into the snow. Long dropped in a white cloth bag, kicked dirt and snow onto it, then thrashed through the brush to the dock just as the little grey tax man reached the cabin. O-da me-tchaw-ne oared his boat briskly out through the floes of ice with Long lumped into the bow as so small a mound, he seemed no more than a flopping trout, eager to be set free. About a half mile out, the boat met the *Queen of the Great Lakes*, returning from delivering mail to the other islands. The smaller boat pulled alongside, hesitated, unhanded its passenger, and rowed back to shore.

A small boy, a child of Elecmantha's scrambled down, then back up the slope on hands and knees and flashed by Samantha, who turned to follow him inside.

She sniffed as she stepped around the Revenue man. She decided the Revenue man stank of rank lagoons with the bones of marsh birds sucked into the peet. Paintable. Were such odors paintable? Sidling next to Elecmantha, she stood at the table at Melissa's head, and laced her fingers through Melissa's frozen hands.

"You can see we have had a tragic death here," Elecmantha spoke firmly.

Marguerite sniffed. "What is that ... odor ... sir? Is that you or Melissa?"

"Yes, ma'am, it is I. Out on the lake two months now following your husband. I have a complaint signed by the Michigan Tax Revenue Service that your husband — that is, Daniel Ben Long?" Marguerite did not answer; Samantha bit her lip. Elecmantha spoke firmly. Marguerite sniffed. "What is that ... odor ... sir? Is that you or Melissa?"

"Yes, Ma'am, it is I. Out on the lake two months now following your tax-evading husband. I have a complaint signed by the Michigan Tax Revenue Service that your husband — that is, Daniel Ben Long?"

Marguerite did not answer; Samantha bit her upper lip. Elecmantha stared at him so hard, his fingers twitched strands of wool from his coat. He addressed Marguerite again. "Ma'am, we believe he's been burying whiskey in a dry county and avoiding the tax, then shipping it out. You don't mind if I look ar ... ?"

Very slowly, very carefully and extremely tall, Elecmantha twitched round the table and looked down into the Revenue man's eyes. He winced, not to be put down by any woman, no matter she stood nearly seven feet and had to stoop six inches to keep from getting her Samson's hair caught on the overhead beams. The Revenue man was not himself particularly tall. He looked at the short black-haired one with the pinched face. Marguerite was no Delilah.

"You can see," Elecmantha whispered, "that there has been an accident." In height and breadth Elecmantha's voice grew, until the little room reverberated and the stove's smoke fled out the window. Her eyes hardened with the force of iron ore, heated to dusk amber.

"I understand, Ma'am, but I'm sent by the Michigan Tax Revenue Department to find a Mr. Daniel Ben Lo ... "

Elecmantha's massive finger touched the only flesh on the

man that was large: his nose. It swelled out of proportion to his body. Its only job, Samantha thought, to sniff out the elusive fumes of lake bound tax evaders.

"You!" Elecmantha's voice held the timber of God's own range sucked up a grizzly's nose, and blown out its throat. She gripped him by his shoulders, pressed his back to the table. He clutched at her hands large as any man's to pull himself up. The back of his head pressed within an inch of Melissa's face. Elecmantha grasped his flailing hands and yanked him up.

"Yes, ma'am?" His voice choked ever so slightly.

"This is NOT a bootlegger's warehouse! This is THE house of God!"

"Er? It is?"

"Look around you. What do you see?"

The man's eyes glanced back and forth across Samantha's colorful paintings splashed up and down the log walls, as if in their colors, somehow, he could remember what the Revenue book had told him about hostile situations. "A ... a ... a ... I don't know."

"A TABERNACLE! Take your tax violations to the politicians where they belong." And in that way, Elecmantha, unknowingly, gave her politician husband away.

◆

The stove burned low toward midnight. Samantha stroked the cold Melissa's head with her fingers. "Wake up," she whispered miserably. Dusk turned to dawn. Still, no one moved. Light rose in the room. Marguerite kicked the table. This jolted Melissa so that her body jumped as if alive. Samantha scowled at Marguerite; Marguerite glared.

"The truth is not even a damn duck could get in and out of

here now 'til May." Marguerite clipped her words out. "Damn lake's freezing again. Not that WE have even a logging boat."

"Throw some logs across, end to end. Ice cracks, at least you're sitting on a log when you go through." Samantha bared her teeth. Marguerite scowled. Elecmantha raised her goddess's head and stared at the boy in her lap. Because at the word "log" he sat up and spoke out, shrill.

"I carved my letters on a log, Mama."

"Shh! We're trying to think. Be quiet!"

"T.L. for Tom Long. That's I. Mama, isn't that me?"

"Yes, now shush so I can think!"

"I couldn't walk, the snow was deep. Daddy lifted me up and set me over on the pile of rocks and snow he'd been shoveling."

"Just for once! Can't you keep that child quiet, El?"

"What's flown into your mouth, Tom?"

"Mama, I was just trying to say, Daddy had to move the log back over the hole where the bag was."

"What bag, Tom?"

"He said he was burying gold and that if I told anyone he'd ... " Young Tom glanced round their faces, eyes filling, then buried his head in Elecmantha's shoulder and sniffed his betrayal to his father's scent, laced into one of Long's old coats bound round his mother.

Samantha stood up and walked out into the dusk of another night.

Clouds trailed the last edges of lapsing light. Wind picked up tendrils from Samantha's hair. She brushed the snow off a stump, and sat stiffly, sorrow in the slump of her shoulders, despair lining her young face.

O-da me-tchaw-ne appeared in her mind. Strange, she thought, he had not uttered one word before he boated Long off. Samantha ached to know how he had found Melissa, an event he had not had time to reveal. Too, she secretly wanted to touch him, and she didn't know why.

From her pocket she drew the gifts Melissa had given her the day they had said goodbye: a four-holed button on a loop of red thread, a hankie with "Samantha" embroidered in pink script, a little doll hardened with peat and two rose petals stuck on for a dress.

Marguerite came up silently behind her. She touched Samantha's hair. Samantha took hold of Marguerite's elbows and jolted her until Marguerite's thin black hair worked free of its bun and flew in wild circles. She rattled Marguerite until Marguerite's hands popped loosely round her wrists. "You let her go! You MADE her go! You didn't like her. She didn't even KNOW where she was going!"

Until Marguerite brought her arms up sharply and knocked Samantha's hands back, saying simply, "I did what I had to."

A slight commotion caused them to turn simultaneously. O-da me-tchaw-ne stood at the cabin door, head down, ear flaps rising in the wind, the wolf Mabel sitting, panting behind.

Marguerite stepped forward. "Thank you for bringing our sister home. Listen, we'll make up a bed of blankets and straw for you in the barn. You won't even have to look at Melissa lying opposite you. We can't bury her until the ground thaws, and only God knows when that is now."

"May fifteenth," O-da me-tchaw-ne sighed, who kept track of dates.

Marguerite beckoned for him to follow her into the cabin for blankets; absentmindedly, the wolf followed. Marguerite felt a nosy nudge in her rear. A shriek shot out the door, and Mabel galloped out after it, ears laid back. Eyes alternating from the door to Samantha, the wolf curled twice and lay in the snow. Samantha picked up the rose petal doll from the ground, reseated herself on the stump, and considered the wolf across from her with tearful empathy.

For a day or two, unwilling to re-approach the cold body of his recently found love nor leave her completely, O-da me-tchaw-ne slept curled with Mabel's nose on his back. It was cold on the doorstep of the Mormon wives. Too religious to sleep in the barn to which they had removed the dead woman, every night he dreamed his body heat thawed Melissa by tucking his arm under her head and holding her close.

Snow slid off the hermit in huge chunks when Marguerite woke him to catch fish before dawn. He happily acquiesced in the fishing, but from sleeping outside his back started to go bad again. Reluctantly, he moved into the barn. It was delightful, like being a hermit again, what with the company being so quiet as it was, undemanding, so beautiful, so close.

O-da me-tchaw-ne dared not touch Melissa lying frozen in the straw, but every part of him ached to kiss her to life.

"I remember a child who had words full of gold?" Marguerite's little yippy face barked out the words at breakfast. Elecmantha looked up from her plate where she was cracking beef bones with her buck teeth.

Marguerite stepped in close to the large woman and leaned up on her toes and hissed into her ear: "Aren't you his mother? Doesn't EVERY mother know how to unlatch the cage to her child's heart? A little sweet maple sugar that sticks to the mouth's roof? Hard taffy culled from the lake? Sweet walnut butter that coats a young mouth with promise, so the tongue leaps out and spills what it knows? Hey?"

Elecmantha eyed Marguerite. She was not a woman who moved quickly, so Marguerite waited, busying herself with stirring the stew. But, not being a woman of great patience, Marguerite soon yipped a little yip and leapt for the door with a bucket in her hand. Within an hour, the bittersweet odor of walnut butter emanated from the churn. Elecmantha raised her massive golden head and with a wink, nodded to her sister in crime, and swooshed little Tom over to his Aunt Marguerite.

Ecstatic at all the attention and sweets he was receiving, little Tom stated only AFTER all the walnut butter was gone, and only AFTER they agreed they could make more, that yes ma'am, he knew EXACTLY where that white cloth bag was buried. Yessirree. He could take them right to it.

A promise for a promise. Sweets for the gold.

Tucking the boy into a sled, Elecmantha and Marguerite and little Tom set out. It was now midmorning, the sun was high, the snow banks no lower than the day before. Samantha was too grief-stricken over Melissa to be of much use. Willingly, they left her behind.

O-da me-tchaw-ne, cleaning lake trout by the back porch, eyed the two women in the snow and the one standing at the door.

Marguerite and Elecmantha trucked out through the heavy snow drifts, lifting their legs high, pushing their toes in until they were thigh-deep. Their process of walking was painful and laborious for O-da me-tchaw-ne to see. Daren't he ask where were their snowshoes?

Not being one to speak this thought aloud, he took his rifle, tracked out, and shot a buck deer. Roasting the sinew over a hot fire, showing how he separated it into strings, O-da me-tchaw-ne found himself in a group teaching the skill of tying snowshoes to three Mormon wives who, for reasons he couldn't figure out, listened. Painstakingly, the women laced sinew to deer bone, yanked the strings out, furrowed the needles through and, by noon, arms out for balance as if treading a high wire, they walked gingerly over the snow, on top, without sinking.

Marguerite and Elecmantha stopped, stunned, then jumped and swung each other out across the snow with gleeful shrieks. But when they went to hug O-da me-tchaw-ne, he shied into the woods without a word, Mabel following, looking back over her shoulder, growling low in her throat.

Coming back along the hill paths, Samantha showed him how she had dyed her snowshoes purple. She was careful not to touch him though she yearned to. O-da me-tchaw-ne smiled. Living on crab apples and nuts and venison, he had the sweetest breath. Samantha sniffed close as she dared. The wolf nudged up to her knee and she reached down absent-mindedly and scratched behind its ears.

"That one!" Tom Long shouted. "No! That one!" His mother marched the boy up to a tree and scouring the snow from the lower branches, glanced at him questioningly. "No," Tom Long stuck his thumb in his mouth. "No, must not be that one. It must be THAT one we buried the gold under! It was in a white bag! I remember I carved my name on the tree. Daddy showed me how."

"Isn't he a teaser?"

"Just like his father."

Exhausted from scraping snow off too many trees, Elecmantha and Tom fell into a bear cave hidden under a downed log. When she rose again, little Tom stayed below. Briefly he showed himself, happily trundling on all fours after the bears, eating what bears eat, set to sleep through the winter. People who visit even now say they hear his voice in the trees, calling from farther along the path, shouting, "THIS one! No, THIS is where the gold is!" Like sirens of the Great Lakes calling men down.

At the beginning of April, at the wives' request, O-da me-tchaw-ne went home. He spent a quiet two weeks at his little cabin on the shore. It did him good. Gads, he said, yap this, yap that, everything in the Mormon house is a discussion.

He stuck peet to fill winter holes in his boat, replaced the anchor, measured by eye what weight the yarn might carry. With holes plugged up and a new top board nailed on, O-da me-tchaw-ne wove his way back through the water. The ice floes bounced more loosely on the lake than they had before. Throwing a rope around the pilings, he tied up at the women's dock.

Marguerite and Elecmantha huddled around O-da me-tchaw-ne, pulling their shawls in close from a wind just giving over to spring.

"You log all the logs you can take and you'll get paid with the money we collect from you carting the lumber down to Leelanau. But! If by-some-strange-chance-you-find-the-gold in the woods, we'll give you a quarter of it for your effort." They spoke in monotones as if he couldn't understand.

O-da me-tchaw-ne was not known for being bright. He could work a hard day, longer than any man, cut more trees than a stouter fellow. But following directions, sounds that zigged into his wind-whipped ears with specific instruction came out cross-hatched, incapable of comprehension, blown around on the waves of his brain. Which is not to say he didn't have one good idea, helped along by Samantha's inventive mind.

Two days later, O-da me-tchaw-ne carted one log down to Leelanau for lumbering. On it were the initials "T.L." In the boat with him were Samantha, Melissa Alyssa Victoria Long, the wolf, and a white cloth bag. In a particularly deep part of water, Samantha nudged the log with the initials over the side.

On the public dock at the mainland community in Leelanau, Captain Frederick Johnson and first mate, Boon, glanced up from their unloading of the Chicago-bound *Queen of the Lakes*. They saw a strange man, half-Jesuit with the look of a Native upon him, a wild beard with hooks and fishnet tangled in it, and two Mormon girls in what had to be a stolen lumber boat. One was alive; one was clearly dead.

With a show of the men's guns, O-da me-tchaw-ne jumped backwards into the water. Samantha stood up and slapped the captain across the face. The wolf leapt snarling for the first mate's throat while the captain pushed Samantha down, raised his flintlock and shot Mabel through the heart.

The men whisked the two girls away over Samantha's loud protest, untangled O-da me-tchaw-ne from the lake reeds gasping and coughing, and tightened him in baling wire. Incarcerating him in the harbor master's wood shed, the two men tossed the heavy cloth bag in after him without once thinking they might want to check its insides. They laid Melissa out on the straw floor of the ice house and padlocked its door twice, as if they thought she might escape.

Samantha was questioned ferociously and repeatedly by members of the Mormon church, a journalist from Traverse City looking for a good shoot-'em-up story, and a politician banging around trying to get the voters' attention with a knock-'em-dead tale. The fact that she said nothing to anyone made the Leelanau community think she had been mistreated. Word went out to Beaver Island that the women had trouble brewing fifty miles south and that the Mormon wives best get down there and take care of their business, which was disturbing the local population.

By the time the two older women arrived, anger had looped round their insides, roping them in so tight, they came spitting with the howls of a single, snarling bobcat. The next day, Marguerite, grown tighter, and Elecmantha grown stronger, arrived in a flurry.

"Hey! In there!" Terrified, O-da me-tchaw-ne kept his tongue inside his mouth. The thin wooden door trembled from their pounding.

"We know you're in there!"

Surrounding the shed, the two wives stomped down the door, and pressed him flat. In a fury they themselves could barely fathom, they sliced O-da me-tchaw-ne's tongue in two for thinking he was telling locals in Leelanau about gold up on Beaver Island, a story they fabricated out of fear that he had. Not side to side, they split his tongue down the middle, front-to-back, so when he talked at all, long after, he spoke with the slur of a serpent, his split words sounding like lies, though every thought was keener to the point than most people's adamantly stated truths.

In their fury, they missed the white cloth bag completely.

Samantha scratched and tore at the captain's hands that tried to hold her, until he backed off. Furious, she packed comfrey into the long cut in O-da me-tchaw-ne's tongue to stop the bleeding, then rose from her knees and banged open the shed door. She strode from house to house, knocking on doors, whispering rumors of gold on Beaver Island and how, if people knew what was good for them, they should best get up there before the gold vanished.

The reporter and politician took the nearest boat for Beaver. The captain let O-da me-tchaw-ne out of the woodshed and took off for the island, too. Marguerite and Elec-mantha leapt aboard the last ship to fight for their right to the gold. The families from the community, too long in this godforsaken north country not to want something for themselves, followed in rowboats and canoes until the town held only two.

Sitting outside the shed on two overturned buoys, Samantha's and O-da me-tchaw-ne's faces glowed warmly in the early spring sun. While the breeze shifted from cold to cool, and snow drifts lowered and puddled around their boots, an inner warmth rose between the two, as intimacy warms and links those who have gone on to find out of sorrow their own hope.

Delicately, wistfully, feathery stitch by feathery stitch, with fingertips so gentle they stroked poor O-da me-tchaw-ne's face nearly to orgasm, Samantha Long laced O-da me-tchaw-ne's tongue together with the tiniest needle she could find. His eyes never left her delicately boned face the entire time, and in his attention to the details of her small nose and blue eyes and the wild red curl of her hair alongside her ears, he would say to her later, slowly and painfully during their love-making, that he never felt the needle at all.

◆

Elecmantha seemed to want to forgive O-da me-tchaw-ne and allow him to stay on Beaver, since, as Samantha suggested, he could not have the gold because why was everyone digging holes all over the island if the gold were in Leelanau? Marguerite wasn't sure since even now through the window, a man dug furiously in the yard after gold. Whose fault was it after all, if not O-da's? But the look in Elecmantha's eye suggested that they might consider their husband's involvement. Standing at their husband's desk, Samantha looked over the deed Long had created that granted him all the lands of Beaver Island. Marguerite was crossing out his name and replacing it with her own.

My mother turned eighteen that spring. She did not argue her share of the island's ownership as she could have. Nor did she argue the fact that Long was still alive and could re-take possession, though both thoughts occurred to her. She stood up instead and paced the small log room, coming to an abrupt halt. I think she changed then, became a woman, where before she had only been a girl. "I remember," she enunciated each word, turning and sweeping both women with her gaze. "You let Melissa walk out on that ice with a blizzard coming, not knowing where she was going. And O-da me-tchaw-ne saved your puny lives from starvation."

Marguerite opened her mouth to retort. Elecmantha stroked her fresh pink skin washed clean by Samantha's tears, and shot Marguerite down with a rib bone she was cleaning of its meat with her teeth. The bone lodged in the dress folds over Marguerite's left breast, as close to the heart as a bone can go.

"All right then," Marguerite held up the bone. "We'll say there wasn't any gold or bootleg whiskey either, and that the tax man was a liar. Oh yes! And that Tom Long didn't know a white cloth bag from a she-bear. But!" And she stroked the left side of her nose with her forefinger. "Being your Native man there is a good wildlife tracker ... and to make up for skipping out on our logging agreement, O-da me-tchaw-ne can stay on Beaver if he does one last thing for us."

O-da me-tchaw-ne, contemplating the body of Melissa Alyssa Victoria Long in his cabin down on the shore, listened silently to Samantha's report. And in a thrall of recent oral pain, O-da me-tchaw-ne agreed to Marguerite and Elecmantha's request. If they wanted him to bring Long back, he would bring Long back. That's what he did for a living: he tracked people. It was one of those things he never asked himself why; it just seemed right concerning what he'd seen happen to the women on Beaver.

A man's wife calls him, a man goes. And he felt proud of that thought. He took it to mean he knew a thing now about married life. And he touched the red curls that lay on the shoulders of the woman he considered his wife.

The legislature's final session closed for the summer. Long

took his leave, riding back north, picking up rumors in Saginaw that a large fellow was after him. So too, the rumors went, was a gang of anti-Mormon politicians, claiming Long owed a full year of taxes for hiding whiskey in a dry county. Much note was made by the tellers of this traumatic news that, though the politicians were out for blood and money, the single fellow on his own was a bear of a man, one of the best trackers in the business. His reason couldn't be discerned by anyone trying to get him to talk. "Off Beaver," they said. "Ain't that where you come from?" Worried the revenuers had hired a gun, Long surrounded himself with highly paid guards.

South of Beaver Island, O-da me-tchaw-ne hid his boat on the mainland in a stand of poplars. Yanking himself by roots up a short steep bank at Neahtawanta, he snuck onto the farm of Mormon Tucker. As Long's two highly paid guards were seeing who could pee the furthest, O-da me-tchaw-ne spotted Long. The tall, thin, severe man was bent over burying crates that rattled with brown bottles, when O-da me-tchaw-ne rushed him. At the same moment, a gang of men holding guns, and a small grey tax man waving a paper, charged out from behind Mormon Tucker's house. In the resulting skirmishes and gunshots, Daniel Ben Long was killed and O-da me-tchaw-ne arrested.

On June 1, the prosecuting attorney for the State of Michigan filed a complaint in the Michigan criminal courts against Theodore P. Stevenson a.k.a. O-da me-tchaw-ne, a hermit of Jesuit and Ottawa blood, to be tried for the murder of Daniel Ben Long, a state legislator and Mormon minister.

On appeal to the second appellate division, many people spoke for O-da me-tchaw-ne, including but not limited to, Samantha Long, former wife of the notorious tax invader, Daniel Ben Long. She testified as to the treatment and starvation of the Beaver Island wives by Long. The Michigan

Revenue Department testified also with profound praise for the hermit who singlehandedly ended Long's long racket of tax law violations regarding the selling of whiskey in dry counties, and the problem of polygamy Long had created in violating the Presbyterian moral code up on Beaver Island.

O-da me-tchaw-ne was acquitted.

In the early autumn, they buried a young woman next to a small cabin on the western shore of Beaver Island. A simple white cross marks the young woman's grave, cut and placed there by the rough, gentle hands and the slender fingers of the simple man and the artist who loved her. In the grave was laid a white cloth bag holding $150,000 in bootleg gold. On it, as on a pillow, rested the head of Melissa Alyssa Victoria Long.

"In this hour of rest, God look down upon you and keep you and hold you. May heaven be warm for you, and these things with which we bury you, stay with you forever, as a token of our love. Amen."

On October 21, under the autumn moon, Samantha Long and O-da me-tchaw-ne were married. They lived an unnotable quiet life on the shore of Beaver Island until the locals rousted up and chased them off in a mass exodus and persecution of the Mormon community among the northern isles.

On Melissa's birthday in the late spring, on Ottawa allotment land owned by O-da me-tchaw-ne's mother, lying slightly north of Reverend Peter Dougherty's New Presbyterian Mission on the Leelanau Peninsula, Samantha Long me-tchaw-ne gave birth to twins, a boy and a girl.

I was the girl.

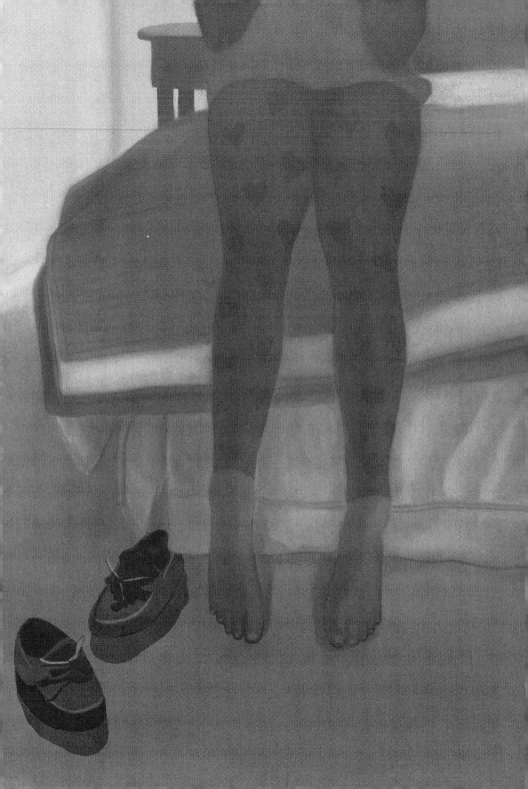

# DEFIANT

It was my mother who found the girl, untied her from the bed and pulled her, filthy and blinking out into the sunlight. I wanted to take her home and give her a bath. She was like a little doll, all blonde, mop-headed and blue-eyed. Dirty, though. She was very dirty.

My mother threw cans of corn and peas, boxes of pancake mix, maple syrup, oranges into the back of the Volkswagen bus. A crate of apples from last fall, I plucked out of cold storage back of the shed, staggered with it out to the car. Handfuls of rice filched from the pantry, my mother's canned string beans, peaches, and beets, we crammed it all into the rear of the bus and rattled heavily down the two track dirt road. We were missionaries on a mission of supreme justice, spies to anyone who asked.

My mother was born generous. Maybe it had to do with being born and growing up in the south. I was probably the only northern Michigan farm kid who knew not to round my "o's." "Pawtsmuth" I went around saying to everyone I knew. "My mother was born in 'Pawtsmuth, Vuhjineea,' and she was educated and had her debutante party in 'Nawfick,'" and I would put my nose into the air and look down it at the plain northern farm girls, until we all broke into giggles and howled on the floor, and tears ran out of our little northern eyes.

It was the grip of my father that attracted her in the first place, she said. And other times she said, "Maybe you've got your temper, and maybe your brother has asthma, but I," she paused so maybe as to weigh whether she should say it, "have your father." If it's true he was a stone around her neck, he was also a rock in the ground and she was the grass which grew around him, shallow-rooted and prolific, for by the time she was done, she'd had eight babies. Billy and I were just the first.

Which is not to say her roots grew deeper; the flowers with which she surrounded herself just grew more numerous. In her mind, I believe she was making little southerners as an act of revenge on the north.

Because in attitude and in bearing and in manners, and in the grace with which she conducted herself, a southerner she stayed. Her generosity in our farming community, through the church and the library, was her privilege and her endowment to those less fortunate, and in her mind all northerners were less fortunate. In her heart, the confederate flag still flew. When people asked about the south, she would raise her arm and wave it in the air and shout, "The South will rise again!"

"I never," my mother said to me over house chores, "had to make my own bed."

"Never?"

"Never. The woman came in twice a week, washed the embroidered sheets, ironed them, and put them back on the bed, polished silver, swept every speck of dust out the door. She did every room in the house; she was a good worker, that woman. Nellie was her name."

"What a lot of work," I said, thinking how I pulled the

covers over my unmade sheets every morning. "How come I have to do it?"

"Because you don't have a nanny."

"How come you got a nanny and I don't?"

"Because your father takes all the money and deposits it in the bank down state."

"Why?"

"If I knew that," she said, pushing her finger through a hole in a sheet, "I'd know why God saw fit to help the north instead of the south."

She leaned against the door until it scraped open with a quick shove, which was just the same as a self-made invitation, my mother said. I didn't think it was right, but my mother stepped in, set the box of food on the hall table.

Dirty kitty litter boxes greeted us in the front hall and the smell of ammonia bouncing around in my stomach reminded me with nausea of my mother's speeding road habits over hills, that little bit of time when you feel the car lift and you know that, like it or not, you're airborne. I didn't have the best of stomachs. My mother's stomach was made from the lead pipe that ran under the road and across to the barn where the cows pushed the clapper down and drank from it. Lead-foot Alice, the men called her. My mother didn't even wrinkle her nose.

The floor held crumbs and the soiled footprints of heavy boots. A little blonde mophead child in yesterday's shorts, of indeterminate sex, sat meticulously coloring the wallpaper in the living room, drawing faces in the petals on the wall. It glanced at us and let us walk by, didn't seem wild.

"We'll look around," my mother said. "She must have been sick for some time."

A dark-eyed boy popped up from behind an overturned easy chair, held our eyes with a toy pistol in hand, and sprinted for the door. I nailed it to the wall, handed it to my mother who pulled it silently in the bathroom, its little mouth clamped shut and it so venomous, it could have passed for a wild west snake.

"Ech! There's dead flies in the sink." But the water ran and the child screamed, came shooting out and gave me a look, despite its face was clean, and hid behind the chair with the stuffing come out of the arms.

My mother stopped and looked at me, puzzled perhaps — that's what I'd say her expression was. She looked very angry for a moment, and then seemed to let it go. Who at, what for, I didn't know.

"Where's the? ... I'm not going alone." She took my hand and we glided quietly into the shadowy hall, where I dropped her hand because a spy for Humphrey Bogart doesn't hold hands with his mother. Wires hung from a light socket overhead. I expected a choked sound, a scream of "Help me!" wherein my mother and I would leap with our Uzis wide open, shoot down drug dealers, hatchet men, molls. No one would dare bar the path of our justice.

Abruptly a dark door banged open. A boy of five or six in filthy clothes jumped out spread-legged and shot us with an M14 squirt gun. My mother ducked. Water flooded the walls. "I'll get him!" I dragged him out from under the bed and threw him in the bathroom and closed the door. He pounded away, shouting things he was too young to know the meaning of.

My mother crouched and looked at me from the far end of the dark hall, but then she reached with her hand, pushed, swung the door wide, and gasped. Her arm went to her mouth, and I leaped in behind her.

The dullness in the girl's eyes was brittle, caught fire, fanned to smoke, and then fled.

◆

There are things that are unspeakable, the red imprint of a hand that stays on the cheek and eye and hardens on the skin, rope burns that rub the wrists raw, the sullenness in a child's eyes. And me, no more than a child myself, I thought I understood it then; I don't understand it at all now.

What is the emotion that turns a parent against a child, the other children against the child? I cannot grasp it. I roll it in my mind like cookie dough, but it does not flatten into conceivable circles, carries no weight. I cannot pinch a half-inch thickness from it, cannot force cutters evenly onto its surface. I have to lump it up and start over, pounding the damn surface to nothing.

It is hard to say how long we stood looking in at the wreck of this child's life, the defecation and urine, the torn clothes, skin so dark from dirt it looked like someone smeared black tractor grease all over her.

As we knelt beside her trying to avoid her teeth and unclipped nails, he came to stand in the doorway. She glanced up, saw him, hung like a whipped dog. My mother quickly untied her, picked her up never minding the stink, for she weighed nothing, and stood in front of James Carl, Sr., her father.

"Move," my mother spoke. It was an even tone, not shouted, but it held all the authority of the church behind it in which everyone knew my mother was so prominent.

I don't know what James Carl, Sr. thought or what he was capable of.

I had anger rising up in me until I thought I would choke on it, and instead tears came to my eyes and I started trembling and half hid behind my mother, ashamed. Of what, for whom, I could not say.

"Move," my mother said, and he did not give ground. The man stood there, belly sticking out from under his dirty shirt, boots with manure on them standing on the bedroom carpet as if he didn't know it wasn't the barn floor. His eyes narrowed on the girl in my mother's arms.

"Katie?" he said. "Come to Papa?"

The girl looked at him for a long, long moment, and I could feel from her arm I was holding she was trembling, but then she seemed to gather herself, rise half-up, her thin body shaking all over. "No," she whispered. That defiance must have cost her because she leaned her head against my mother's chest and closed her eyes.

My mother did not move. "I will not ask you again," she said. "In God's name, you do what is right now."

And James Carl, Sr., who could have beaten my tiny mother to a pulp, stepped back, spun on his manured heel and strode out, swinging the bedroom door wide behind him, as if in the end, he knew we were going to go through and take the girl out.

"How could I say," my mother said to my father when he came in at six from the orchard, "that she knew art, had heard music, understood the flight of swallows to Henderson's cliff? Why should I say that she was better off tied to that bed post than with a good family, a good home?"

"It's not our business," my father said. "It's got nothing to do with us. Leave it alone." But his eyes lingered on her, caught by something he could not name, held, until he did not look away. Something came into his face: an idea, perhaps, a recognition fanned by the July wind that took on strength, blew open a gate in his mind. "Where is she?" he whispered. He abruptly stood to his feet. "Alice? Where is the child?"

And my mother, in the boldest move we had ever seen her make, flung wide the doors to our parlor which had long since been turned into a second nursery, and reached in with both arms and pulled the girl out. Filthy and nasty as a wild barn cat, she fought my mother's embrace. I dared not breathe.

"I will not have! ... "

"David Simon Jackson, you will have and you will listen to everything I have to say and when I'm done you will do nothing and say nothing. This is my affair. I made the choice to bring her away from there."

"Go!" she said to us and we were so used to her not raising her voice to us, that we stood rooted, stunned, then turned and fled, secretly happy that someone had finally spoken to our father that way.

Within three days, my mother and I took the girl before Judge McCrea who pronounced her a ward of the court. He leaned over the bench in his black robe, asked my mother would we take her in as a foster child? My mother sighed, and started to cry. The judge shooed the other people out of the courtroom and rose behind his bench and shrugged out of his black robe and came and put his arms around my mother and comforted her, for more time than I thought I could bear.

The girl and I sat at the table behind them, our heads down. I was embarrassed and I didn't even know what I was embarrassed about. I scraped the wood table with my thumbnail and drew tic-tac-toes and nudged her arm to play. She sat silently, blank in her eyes, as if she were dead. As if she did not care. As if the world were all the same to her, foster home, parents' home, what was the difference? One was just like another. I tried to pinch her.

"I'm sorry, Noel," my mother whispered, "you know he won't." Judge Noel McCrea patted my mother's shoulder and kissed her cheek, and returned to the bench. He called for the court officer who went out and came back in immediately with a thin woman wearing a suit and a pretty smile.

"Social worker," my mother whispered to us. The pretty woman signed papers at the judge's desk and spoke gently with the girl at length while my mother and I gathered our things.

Katie was sent back home with the social worker, cleaned up and dressed in one of my dresses. I wonder what kind of shreds it's hanging in now, wonder more often about my mother and the judge. But I can't say I knew anything for sure.

◆

I couldn't sleep. I kept thinking James Carl, Sr. would come through my window with the stink of manure on his boots and do to me what he had done to Katie only worse, as if I really knew what he had done.

My mother went light on me, smiled at me more than usual, touched my hair and offered to talk. But when I sat down at the kitchen table and looked at her, nothing came out of my mouth.

I was never a gentle child, never a predictably sweet girl with dolls and manners, but the day we let that girl go back home, I transformed over night, clenched my fists and swore and spit as rough as any of our hired migrant boys swinging and drunk for a fight on Friday night with money in their pockets and whiskey in their minds. I was thirteen years old. I turned away from people, fled into hiding places in the woods if anyone dared come near me.

But I couldn't stop my thoughts, I couldn't change them, couldn't shrug them away. They had to come, toppling over each other. Exhausted, I gave up struggling, standing beside my mother on the darkening porch, stunned.

Because of us, the church converged on the Carls like ants on peanut butter. You couldn't stop them, couldn't unstick them, couldn't flick them off. The cars went by our house breakfast, lunch, and dinner, bumping down the Carls' road, one or two or three at a time.

We walked down to see, stood in the first row of orchard trees, saw as they handed in clothes by the basketful, food by the aluminum pan. They moved into the Carls', swept floors, washed laundry, gave the children daily baths and prayers, and so undid the natural order of the Carls' daily life that James Carl brought his insane wife home, stood shotgun at his door on the fourth morning, let his children pelt the church people's cars with stones.

But it is we who opened their door, and the church, in its mission, which followed and pressed down, drowned the Carls' voices, squashed their ability to put their lives back together, to try and do right by their own.

And I'm not saying the Carls were good and decent people. Everything I know about the Carls goes against it. But to be made into public victims and felt sorry for is to shred a family of any attempt to raise themselves in the public view, to bring back self-respect, to re-create a decent life from the shambles of the old one, to say yes, we made a mistake. Because then there is no family.

And that was our crime.

# TO OWE DEATH

# A LIFE

It's been twenty-four years since the water dropped a hundred feet in this bay and a lighthouse was built on Devil's Island; twenty since water rose up its walls and covered its blinking tip. But who can say when the water lifts and lowers in this bay? Some years twice a year? Others once a lifetime? I wish it were a lie. I wish it never happened, but I tell you straight and true.

The last time the lighthouse rose from the bottom of the bay was last January, the month of the two-faced moon. It cracked through the ice, rose straight up in one morning, and the year was last year, and the day was today, and the light in the tower was turning in slow broad blinks.

For the Mormon gold Henry and Notso stashed in the sinking lighthouse, Henry agreed to a poker game: five-card stud, jacks wild, five hands, winner take all. On the stone floor of the lighthouse, when it rose. Go ahead. Ask Notso. He swore to it on Henry's drowning screams that if anyone asked, he would say what he saw.

You see, its not where Henry is now that matters; it's the honorable thing. Did they or didn't they *each* owe Death a life? And once the two started playing, were they playing on even ground?

◆

But for a thickly curled red beard and a stubbly red patch around his private parts, Henry's fishing partner was bald from head to toe. He had certain important failings, too: his clumsy giant's hands were not sensitive on the bait lines. A thirty-five pound lake trout steered their leaky five horse-power rowboat sixteen miles north and twenty coming back, before Notso had the good sense to look up. His true failing was that he had to be told to do things he he'd done seven times before. That's why people called him Notso, so they could say: *Notso Bright are ya?*

In contrast to Notso, Henry was small, lean in frame, hands sensitive on the bait lines, hair the hue of angels. Half the size of his fishing partner, his success *and* his failing was that he had a mouth born out of that little yellow hole near the tail end of the fish where the guts come out in the clean-ing: sometimes dark as the devil's tongue, sometimes sweet as pie.

Henry had a quality to his voice, range and depth, a light-ness, a gift to make people understand what they hadn't yet figured out what they were doing in this life, for which most people have no common sense. When Henry talked, you could point to yourself and say, sure, that's right, *now* I see. Had he been of a different temperament, Henry could have been minister to a church congregation, the savior of souls, the grace-sayer of those crossing to eternity. But a temper flared up in him, born of a long-standing sense of inadequacy.

---◆---

With women, he was pitiful. The precious tones faltered, for not being more of the kind of man who understands women at some deep level some men understand ... or the kind of man whom women would want to touch. He blamed it on being small in his body parts, missing, therefore, in his own arguments, the very thing most crucial about himself: not the size of his penile member, but the size of his *shyness*. What he lacked in social abilities, he lacked only with attractive women. Ugly ones he could sometimes manage.

It became not unusual to see Henry pulling Notso out the tavern door by his collar with a woman brandishing an armed weapon after. You might have thought it would be the other way around: Henry pulling Notso out the door to save Notso's dumb life.

But women flocked to Notso's quietness. They begged him to slip their tongues between his teeth. They touched him in his largeness, planted themselves over the size of him. They didn't mind that Notso clinked and clanked with tin cups and fish filleters strung from his coat, bear knives, beaver traps, wolves' teeth, the petrified tail of a lake trout, the rattle of Petoskey stones in his pockets, no. He merely moved these accouterments aside, and pasted themselves on him.

Notso, looking at Henry, would grin, shrug, disappear into a back room or under the bar, or on the pool table or on the back side of a door from which the grunts and gurgles and yelps would issue.

Had Notso been another man, Henry might have lashed his words around the big man's head, tied the knots tight and dashed his partner's face to the ground. But with Notso, though he could have, he didn't. What one man allows in one and not another, I can't say. Some men fit.

Together they make one man.

———————◆———————

With the war effort on, people working on the great lakes were rounded up by the U.S. Navy Department and put to work on the Great Lakes' freighters, hauling coal and iron ore, wood to rebuild the nation's cities.

No animosity curled between Notso and Small Henry. Notso did the heavy work while Henry ran howling orders to the men, his voice pitched to rise above Lake Superior's gale winds. Notso had his own success: winning praise from the men for running from the wheelhouse to the stern with a two hundred and fifty pound box of rifle shells balanced on his head.

So when the ship EMPEROR, carrying 10,429 tons of natural iron ore, sailed into Lake Superior's early morning darkness and took on water, Notso yanked the unconscious captain from the fallen mast and wrapped his arms around the side of the lifeboat and held them both on until the U.S. Coast Guard cutter arrived. On the THOMAS BANNON, Henry pushed Notso into Lake Michigan as a streak of red fire leapt out of the hold and kindled an arc in the air from a million gallons of crude oil burning that sunk the ship to the lake's glacial floor in twelve seconds.

Henry was an officer, Notso a freight man. They were captain and recruit, overseer and underling. In weight, Notso could have crushed Henry with his fingertips, but Henry spoke words that expressed to others what was in Notso's heart. Notso knew they were words he could never utter because his vocabulary was so weak, comprised only of a

———————————————

few grunts and groans and an occasional laugh. And in that way they got along in the world, one looking out for the other.

You could say that death stalked them, but you could say perhaps it didn't stalk them any more than it stalked any other man who lashed his life to the Great Lakes' freighters. That one hundred twenty-three ships went down in Superior in one year was no light number. You could almost think it was intentional, though no one's made the case. Who would they make it against? God?

◆

In 1948, in the shattering winds of an ice storm, a tanker off South Manitou Island rolled under. Three times it swung up, its decks trying to surface; three times it swung down again, until the third time, the ballast flooded and it sank in six hundred feet of water.

The lighthouse keeper and his wife on Manitou searched the shoreline long hours for survivors. After two weeks, they gave up and radioed their unsuccessful results to the Coast Guard commander in Traverse City. One month later, two men crawled across the snow and sleet and solid ice of the passage between the islands and the mainland and threw themselves against the lighthouse door: Henry and Notso, remnants of that broken ship. Behind them they dragged a trunk of Mormon gold.

The most anyone could say is: they each owed Death a life.

The second to last thing happened in midsummer last year and there's no accounting for it to have caused a death. But that's the way death works: it takes you when you're doing something stupid. It never takes you when you're acting with common sense. Which isn't to say that the one time you're doing everything right, Death doesn't lift up its hand and knock you down.

◆

Gill nets and shiny new size six hooks, minnow buckets, anchors, new oarlocks and a slightly used five horse-powered motor went into their old rowboat from the ships wages they'd saved and they fished together from the Leelanau peninsula.

Then last year, they pulled a 1960 Chevrolet Biscayne car out of a ditch back behind the state forest in the town dump. They cranked it up on siphoned gasoline, surprised that the darn wreck still ran.

"I'm driving first." Notso thumped his big barrel chest.

"You touch that car and you'll be a flying tin can hanging from the bumper."

"It ain't got no bumper."

"That's 'cause you knocked it off in the ditch."

"I'm driving!"

"Twos wild, man with the axe, the Jack of Hearts, winner drives first on a five card draw. It's now or never."

In the fishermen's tavern, at the bar, Henry bet the driver's seat and drew four cards. Notso laid one down, picked one up.

"Show."

"Fine!" Notso banged his hand down. "I'm just gonna go sit in it." He thumbed his nose up. "People who pull outside straights on all four cards ought to be gutted from that little yellow hole on the bottom of the fish where the guts come out in the cleaning." Which is to say, sometimes, Notso had words.

Henry, an excellent notcher of cards, jumped off his stool,

opened the tavern's door, slammed it behind him, trundled down to the bay where he crouched into the rocks and sand and began retying fishing nets they'd spread out on the rocks on the beach in the morning to dry. Inside the tavern, we could hear him muttering and sighing.

Notso bolted through the back door, stomped through the weeds and gravel and leaned against the Biscayne. He scuffed a batch of pine needles around on the ground with his boot, whistled a little tune to the squirrels in the jack pines overhead. He counted to five by missing two, three and four, then cranked open the solid black door of the Biscayne. Notso was a raccoon on the rim of a stuffed garbage pail.

The big smooth steering wheel, the solid steel dash of a 1960 black Chevy Biscayne. Notso smiled. It was gold, he thought. Gold. And the day's so nice.

He turned the key. The big motor powered up with a slow chug-chug. His big toe tap-tapped on the gas pedal, but there was no increase in rev from the motor. He looked around at the instruments on the dash, but having no education but fishing, he could not read what they said. Angry at his own stupidity, he stomped his entire foot to the gas pedal, then pushed it to the floor.

The car roared, the engine raced, the wheels backspun on sand. Notso banged the gear shift down with his knee and the big car crunched forward on gravel. With a sudden whiff of gasoline, the car lurched clattering out onto the road.

Now the engine idled so high Notso didn't have to put the gas on. He laughed. Ha-ha. And again, Ha-Ha! And again, Ha-ha-ha! Six miles out on the old highway, he took a side road and pulled up in front of a house trailer, where he let the car idle under a big maple,

Jessie Mae sat in her pink short shorts with her lean legs up on the step to a house trailer. Wiping the sweat and dust and long blonde hair from her eyes, she rose and ambled over, leaning into the driver's side window and kissing Notso so long and hard he almost stopped breathing.

"Like to take a ride up M-72 to Empire with me, Jessie Mae?"

Jessie Mae smiled a heart-wrenching smile, she was just eighteen. She glanced sidelong back at the trailer, and climbing through the car window, crawled over top of Notso where she sat down on him, straddling her legs up alongside his bald head. Notso grinned, pressed the gas on hard and drove with two hands on either side of her, holding the steering wheel, peering through her blowing hair while Jessie Mae fitted her hips exactly to his.

With the windows open and the hot air gusting in, the car rattling at fifty miles an hour, Jessie Mae undid her shirt. Her long white fingers trailed from the last button, and Jessie Mae lifted her arms up. The shirt hurtled out the open window and flew behind them, where it drifted and settled to the empty road behind.

At the magnificent sight of Jessie Mae's naked breasts, Notso drove the car into a ditch on the side of the road, bounced it up out of the dirt at forty-five miles an hour, careened it into the state forest, scraped the bark off two large oaks, and *slammed* the car down over a good-sized boulder beneath a great jack pine. Taking a breast in each hand, he nuzzled Jessie Mae, while she reached down between them and unzipped a certain place in his clothing..

The point of the rock the car had landed on sat up under the hot rocking brakes.

The car began to bounce, first a little, with just the seat springs creaking, then louder and harder it rocked, until it was not just up and down, but back and forth the car rocked over that boulder, up and down, back and forth, granite rock rubbing heat into the overheated brakes until hot desire so flooded Jessie Mae, she fell over on the seat and moaned into

Notso Bright's hairless chest: "My Puppy, you're some lover that you can make love so hot you're smoking."

Notso lifted his head slowly from her hair. Sniffing, he reached over her head, slammed down the door handle and whanged open the car door, which creaked and groaned and cracked on its rusty hinges, upon which the entire door thudded to the ground. Flames sprang up from under one wheel and a blue smoke winged its way up into the front seat.

"Sheee-itt!"

Wearing Notso's shirt on her, Jessie Mae leaned over to pick up her own shirt from the road, dropped his and walked on, but paused once, looking back to see him standing there in the weeds on the side of the road, massive arms crossed over his hairless chest, watching the flames engulf the car. She turned then and came back, picked up his shirt, flung it around her shoulders and went on up to Empire, her long blonde hair fluttering in the hot breeze.

What little mind there was in Notso Bright's head did not perceive the danger of fire, nor no longer the smell of smoke. In his deeply sensuous nostrils, Notso smelled Jessie Mae's long perfumed hair and her Ivory soap skin, and then he groaned, loud and deep and long.

It was Henry's fault that the car didn't run right.

And he took off, lunging through the state forest, snapping branches off trees, striding rapidly over fallen tree trunks, straddling gullies and pushing their cliff edges wider apart. Or at least, that's the way it seemed to those who heard the tale later and imagined it in their minds, what minds they had after they came out of the tavern. He marched down the big embankment to Lake Michigan in such leaping bounds that it seemed, given his size, that when his feet landed, the water in the lake trembled and rose. Pounding down the rocky shore, he walked his furious way back to Kenegun, half-naked, damn near burnt, and slammed his giant hands down on the fish gutting table out back of the Tavern, where Henry was eyeing a fifteen-pound black bass in the eye, a pair of pliers holding a hook he had just twisted out of the fish's throat.

◆

Henry looked surprised at the fractured table. Notso spit a huge glob of drool. It landed on Henry's boots, the only part of his clothing he kept shiny.

"Your damn car aint' worth a fish's ass; it nearly killed me and Jessie Mae!" Notso took his partner who was no longer his partner, by the throat and closed his powerful hands around it. We thought the end had finally come, and all tripped over each other racing out to see.

Henry, who was quick with his wits, being smaller and at a disadvantage against his larger fishing partner, aimed the pliers and buried the number six hook so deep into Notso's beard it arced through Notso's cheek.

"The fish ... is caught ... by the hook ... in its mouth," Henry gasped out against Notso's hands.

Notso stared at Henry. He swung his head to the right, but the razor edge of the hook scraped against his cheek. He undulated his head back to the middle, feeling the hook bite again. Blood seeped from his cheek. His hands loosened on Henry's neck, and Henry fell.

When Henry sprung up, it was with a hard board, splintered from the gutting table. With glee, he whacked Notso in the head, and leapt back.

Notso shut his mouth and refused to open it. Henry, never one to miss a dealt hand, followed suit. And neither one nor the other spoke until winter.

Some men I'd've said, work together too long. From two

they should be one. And for once, they all looked at me and nodded their heads.

———————◆———————

January, and the bay to the Great Lakes froze two feet thick, patched over with half-frozen ice fishing holes, treacherous to wander near, deadly to step into.

For no good reason we could figure in the Tavern, Notso leapt up and stood tottering on the bar stool, shouting at Henry.

"I know you got Mormon GOLD stashed on Bassett Island! You showed it to us right here last summer! You stole it off North Fox, you SAID, and you were going out to HIDE it on the island when the lighthouse came up through the ice! And don't say you didn't! I saw you right here in the tavern open the damn trunk! And I saw someone come in and I saw you close it and go out and put it in the car and drive off and come back without it! Well, I know it ain't in your car because gold don't burn."

"Tell him," Henry nodded to Eliza behind the bar. "That I can whack him into a thousand little pieces with this fish gutter."

"Tell him yourself."

"You think I couldn't?"

Henry growled, slammed down his coffee cup which broke in two pieces, and looked Notso in his red eyes. "We'll go out there. We'll *wait* for the island to rise. We'll *go in* that damn lighthouse, and *play* five hands for the Mormon gold, since you insist."

"Fine!" both men stood, arms crossed, chests huffed up, each one righteous with indignation.

"Boys?" Because all men were boys to Eliza, who stood

before them, head cocked to the side. "Don't you think you ought to wait until rumor says the bay is washing out and the island is rising? How long you going to sit out there on the ice freezing your asses until the sandbar gives out?"

Notso slurped his coffee down. Henry turned his head. Both rose and left the tavern.

One year ago, today.

But I tell you straight and true. For the Mormon's bootleg gold stashed in the sinking lighthouse, Henry agreed to a draw. Five card stud, jacks wild, six hands, winner take all. Go ahead. Ask Notso. He can't lie. He swore to it, through Henry's drowning screams that he would tell what he saw.

Rumors fly on the wing, fluttering one way, whispering the other, and each time the story gets changed, so people get it all wrong, so it comes out differently, full of sticks and nickels, racoon meat from a bobcat's body.

The lighthouse was up, it was down, it was flying, it was round. It was a duck, with a bald head, a burning car, a deck of notched cards. It was a girl's long lean legs draped out of the window of a black 1960 flat-finned Chevy Biscayne.

The winter twilight lay bright on the meadow. Twenty or more people rose from their seats in the tavern and followed the two men out. The door was rimed with ice and the moon cast a pale blue glow over all.

Two men filed under the stark-branched trees of the orchard, crossing the twilit meadow. Pricker branches arching out of the snow snagged the thighs of their pants as the two men eased out onto the rim of West Grand Traverse Bay. The bay cracked and heaved beneath their feet. No trick of night's light, the ice on the bay sat breathing. Up, and down, it rose; up-and-down.

Twenty-five miles of drifting snow lay ahead: flat and frozen, spreading its skirts five miles from one side of the bay to the other. At the northern tip, beyond two points of land lay the lake, where the tumultuous waters of Lake Michigan never freeze.

Tentatively, one looking one way, one looking the other, they stepped out onto the ice. The people from the Tavern stamped their feet, blew on their hands leaned like a picket fence along the shore, hooting and hollering and egging them on. I sunk back into the shadows of the cherry trees, hiding from what I'd been asked to do.

I'm an old man; I don't care for fights, I don't need to know why people quarrel, but Eliza had been saying to me that I needed some way to be useful. I thought being an old man I'd used up all my uses. But I was asked to go, to record in my mind what I saw, and come back to tell it. And they pushed me out on the ice, calling me: the Teller of True Tales, the Teller of False Lies, because some lies are truly false and yet some truths you can't trust with a lie. And then ... I was bound to it.

You understand the truth? The island comes up when water in the bay washes out through the sand bar and into Lake Michigan. One nudge sometimes, and the whole dune goes like a sand castle on the beach with one wave. This usually happens during spring thaw, but the lake *is* unpredictable: it could happen *any time* when the water in the bay is high enough. And the water was high.

When it happens the bay washes out in a magnificent rush into Lake Michigan, foaming and feuding at that place where a straight line slices from the Leelanau Peninsula's northernmost point across West Bay to the point at Old Mission, and if you could walk that line, you'd be walking the 45th parallel and wondering, if somehow, it were holy for dying.

◆

We carried no fishing nets, no string for gilling, no bait for hook lines. Ne-tche-wod, dark snow clouds left their cargo behind to trail us, while the night sky shifted, became Wa-zhe-tou-tchig awsh-kou-te, the aurora borealis, they that make fire in the sky.

Six hundred feet beneath our boots the bones of the lake freighters and the crews who oared them lay writhing in the muck. We trod lightly, lifting our boots to the wind, stepping as if we were three children walking on cracking ice, because that's what we were: *three-grown-children-walking-on-cracking-ice.*

We toted one deck of new cards, one deck of old, slung in a burlap sack over Henry's right shoulder, so no one could finger them, mark them, turn the corners down before the game and know — when he went to bet — what cards had already been played.

Henry walked ahead, taking the brunt of the wind, his eyes cast down to the dark slushy surface of the ice. Ten feet to the east, Notso clanked with pots and pulleys, oarlocks and anchor ropes.

Icicles froze to tree limbs, yet dripped from their melting tips. Small creatures stared up through the ice, google-eyed. Frozen in the ice, they seemed to blink. Beneath our feet the surface warmed and melted. Fissures and ripples broke through and hissed, as if the ice were breaking up. Although we stopped often, listening for ice breaking, we heard nothing but the rising wind. Though I turned around to look many times, there was nothing following but my own fear, the shadow of the Bearwalker: Death itself tracking someone we walked with.

Henry's face was red with cold. Glancing aside at Notso from time to time, eyeing each other like two old wolves passing parallel in the night on the other's territory.

The truth was they'd been at each other's throat since the war ended. Once they'd settled into fishing after the freighter work, they'd quarreled over who'd bring the fish nets in, who'd take the fish nets out. They had fought up and down the bay, all their working lives: did they need the second ice-fishing hole over by Elzer's? No, maybe it should be back by Marion Island.

Yap, yap, yap.

I would have closed my ears if I'd had a key and each ear were a door. Like old fish they were, rushing in to bite the same dead worm. Silences, I could have said to them, speak louder than words. But I *didn't* speak, and maybe that was my failing.

You see, I'd fished with them on and off for twenty years, and even *I* didn't know what they were fighting about. A girl this time? An old beat-up car with a back seat that laid down? A trunk of Mormon gold?

*Come on.* The gold was an awakening, a knock on the face of stupidity. Time to quit fishing together; but they let it be the decider of two lives that had lived as one and would now split apart, were about to come fully asunder.

I turned my back on them once they got started; I would have flown from their squabbling to another shore in a distant state, but I was an old crow with tattered wings and few choices. So I closed my mouth, though it went against my nature. Kept my tongue against my teeth and took to humming to drown out the sounds of their unwhispered contentions.

◆

When I couldn't stand their petty grievances anymore, I set my boots to crunch across the ice closer to shore and made my way up across the sand and onto the rocks and into the dense trees, where at least the snow and ice and frozen limbs, in the blackening night, were quiet.

Maybe there were words said between them out there on the ice, whole sentences or partial phrases that could tell us what happened. Words that could point to one choice or another that was made, so we could know what truly occurred, but I cannot recount to you their every word because I chose not to translate their words into mine.

How much can one person know about the thoughts and reasons of another.

I knew where they stopped. I knew what place lay beneath their feet.

It was an old familiar ice fishing hole near over Neahtawanta, on the east side of the bay, under a long overhand of frozen branches where we'd caught lake trout earlier in the season: one twenty-five pound lake trout and one fifteener. But there was more to it.

They were standing over the site of Devil's Island. Under the ice lay a small island with a small lighthouse on it. And there was no sign of either protruding. No cracking of ice, no dropping of water, no blinking light coming up like the Devil's spire, the Catholics among our people would say, fed by natural gas. Though the ice's surface had remained sloshy our entire trip, except in the beginning when it had seemed to breathe like some huge beast, there was nothing. And I looked behind me, because old men get like little children: fearful and superstitious.

And who believes such things but children who've seen too little and old men who've seen too much? Ask anyone, they'll deny it. They'll say it's just not true, water doesn't lower and islands don't rise. Who'd believe me? That's all there is to it, God decreed it so, the religious among us say. And he wouldn't want it any other way. But these religious, they're holding certain truths tight to their minds and can't let them go to embrace others. So they're not really good sources for information.

Me, I'm given to think things aren't always what they seem. Life passes us surprises and we're supposed to nod as they go by, not close our eyes and say no, this doesn't exist.

———————◆———————

From his fishing pack, Henry pulled a curled stand of iron he'd forged with a handle on the top and a spike in the end, and set to twisting it into the ice, turning it like a hand-turned drill as if to make a hole so tiny, only an ant could climb up through. Maybe he thought if he broke the ice the lighthouse spire would come up through it. I don't rightly know what he thought. He muttered to himself, too, whistled a tune, off key, scuffled his boots around in the snow on the ice, bent over and brushed the snow off, and tried to peer into the water past the ice.

Notso yanked an axe from his belt, knocking Henry off the little pin prick Henry had dug and began hacking the surface of the bay with his axe.

Two stupid men, I thought, not one, and turned and walked back to shore.

I built a small fire onshore, shot a beaver, skinned and roasted it, tucked the tail in my pocket for good luck and sat, watching two men out on the ice. I was sucking on the bones, wishing I had a full stomach of deer meat, when I noticed the two of them were standing, staring due north, where all things that aren't supposed to be here go.

The air was snap-clean cold, the silence more silent than night. I walked out to the men, treading gently, assuming the ice might be weak for reasons I couldn't understand. Caution was my creed. Still, crack lines rippled in tiny runners, beginning due north and running south back behind my boots, widening, minute by minute, passing by me and going on. The sound I heard was a little rupture and then, a *hiss,* as if the water had held its breath, then let go and come up through the ice, grateful to breathe. This, at the height of pe-boon, winter. But this is what the great lake is: unpredictable.

I was shivering now, though every winter night of my life I've spent fishing out on the ice, immune to cold or snow or sleet. I have no explanation of what I saw next, except fear, by which I mean the shadow of the Ojibwa Bearwalker was tracking right behind us.

I fess up now. And this is it: I tell stories about lighthouses rising that I'd only heard secondhand, never even knowing the truth. Because what's the truth? And what's a lie? That's how I got the name, the teller of true tales, the teller of false lies, because tales are never quite true, and yet a lie is never entirely false. Because I never let a lie slip by without examining it for some detail of truth. Truths, you see, are the cast lines to lies, and lies are shallow brook trout running upstream to spawn in the lake of the truth.

So I am left to tell you only what I saw. Believe it or don't. I am an old man, and many choose not to, though I have outlived many who lied.

The night was bright. In the flat spectral distance, the ice lay all cracks and fissures, the moon basking blue over the glistening snow. It was beautiful, haunting, spectral and dark.

It was that moment that the ice chose to speak.

The ice heaved itself up like mountains rising, and the lighthouse rose, the length of a small pine branch one minute, the height of a large buck deer the next, some moments no more than the width of a small round stone. Through the spray of moonlight and the shifting of colors in the aurora borealis, the lighthouse shot up like buildings on reservations with loan money for casinos. Dark water drained off its green muddy sides, washed over the granite stone floor, ran over the still frozen rocks and thawed them, and down through the lake weed tangled at its base. It washed off the pale tower until we could all see the light in the lighthouse tower turning in slow, broad blinks.

Ask the Methodists, they'll tell you the light was turning and blinking with the breath of drowned Catholics. But ask the Catholics, they'll tell you theirs is the only truth, that the light spins to remind the Methodists they have not suffered enough.

Some people along the shore say a day at best, others say it stayed the night and sank promptly at dawn. But only those who entered the lighthouse knew for certain: that the light was powered by natural gas that the oil companies can't get license to drill for in the bottom of the bay, for it shone over all the wet mud walls of an ancient civilzation that had been abandoned some thousands of years ago.

Ask me, I'll tell you it's the Bearwalker's tongue, coated with peat, lit with the fireballs of a natural fire from two men's lies.

I crept across the ice which rose in spikes and spears, jumping from one ice berg to the next, and I was grateful for being an ice fisherman then, as I was an experienced ice walker.

◆

On the floor of the lighthouse, playing on a trunk spilling with Mormon gold, Notso Bright and Henry laid down their fishing gear and sat to a game of five card stud: jacks wild, five hands, winner take all.

They would have dealt five hands or more for love of the game, but how could they know how much time they'd have? Minutes or seconds, an hour? Does history tell us how long a lighthouse stays up, before the water comes thundering back into it?

But a hand dealt means the game must be played out; it's the honorable thing. What man would risk losing in shame? So you see: it's not whether Henry was right or wrong, it's whether he did the honorable thing.

Did he or didn't he owe Death a Life?

Five hands. Winner take all.

◆

In the time the island stopped rising, they changed the rules. Five card stud, wild were a pair of twos, one-eyed jacks, the man with an axe, winner take all.

Henry pulled cards from his pack, shuffled, re-shuffled, nudged the pile across the table. Notso split the deck. Those cards sparkled; they lit up by the moon's stark gaze, the middleman.

First hand, Henry laid down three, drew two, drew one more, laid the cards down flat and tapped the table with his thumb. Notso threw one, took one and held. Henry nodded. Notso turned over two pair, queens and nines, thumbed his chin to his partner. Henry picked up his cards, turned them over one by one, scattered them across the table. Full house.

Notso's face blinked red; he slammed his fist down on the top of the trunk and creased it. He took a bottle from his pack and waved it at Henry. Henry took a drink. Notso shook his head. Henry dropped the bottle between his thighs.

Notso dealt the cards for a second hand. The cards rattled, jumped a little, skidded across the trunk. A stone fell from high up inside the lighthouse and bounced across the lake's floor with a hollow knocking as it stopped at the lighthouse door, then stopped. Henry heard, listened, paused for a second, as if to follow the sound, saw me, but made no movement, said nothing, and held wild on a pair of twos.

I stood in the door, too terrified to run, too terrified to stay.

Notso leapt up and slammed his fist against the jagged rock wall. He stood there, busted hand against the wall, taking deep breaths, and then swung around, seemed to open his mouth, as if to say something to Henry, but closed it again and instead, pulled the bottle from Henry's thighs, opened it, offered it, and didn't drink himself. Henry drank.

Eliza told me later that the people on the shore counted the time, knowing how long it takes to deal, how many seconds to throw down cards, take two more.

Some whispered it would be the honorable thing to do to stop that game. Some said no. They're not just playing each other, not just playing for Mormon gold or an old bet, or for some wrong that happened a long time ago. When you go to a place like that to lay our your differences, you're playing Death, life's true partner; you *can't* back out.

The lighthouse shook, trembling like a newborn baby. Water rose and leveled, then rose again up the foundation to the slate floor, the trunk bouncing between their boots. Who knew what was in it? Ice and sand? Bottle caps, fish bones, a child's Petoskey stone treasures, the skull of a Pleistocene trout? Who knew?

Third game and Notso refused to cut. Henry took a shot from Notso's whiskey and passed the bottle over the trunk; but Notso kept his cards pressed tight to his chest, refused the drink.

And maybe not drinking was the dishonorable thing, because that put them on separate and uneven ground. In a game against Death, all things must be equal.

One by one, Henry laid down: a queen, two sevens, the one-eyed jack, an ace.

Notso opened the whiskey bottle and placed the rim against Henry's lips, but his hand trembled, as if he would have rather smashed it against Henry's head. Or his own.

◆

Water flooded their boots. Large shards of ice swirled past them in the rising water, clinking and rubbing along the lighthouse walls until they spun across the room in the turbulent dark. Cards danced on the table. The iron ore of the island shook violently. The sound of splintering stone split the air.

Notso eyed Henry with narrowed eyes, waiting for Henry to pick his cards up for the fourth game, but Henry's chin was on his chest. Notso reached across the trunk and lifted one of Henry's cards. Henry leapt up, banged his fist down on Notso's giant hand, and warily, and a little blurry-eyed, turned over a six, a five, a nine, a king, one two, for the fourth game.

Notso smiled and showed an outside straight, but Henry was snoring sound asleep.

The lighthouse slipped five feet in two breaths. Ice water

splashed to the top of the trunk while the cards trembled with the heave and push of the island going down. The water hovered, slapping at the rim of the trunk. The island was rocking now, and Notso's boots were filling with winter water and he didn't snatch the bottle from between Henry's thighs and drink.

Notso Bright was a slow man, especially when his luck was low. He knew a bad day from a good one, when the moon was radiant he ran high. When it was black, he crawled into his cabin on the eastern shore of Beaver Island and waited for the moon to wax toward full to emerge. Now he stood up and strode through the water, and glanced at the snow coming down, and the moon that wasn't there because the dark clouds of storm had gathered over the great lakes. And he made a decision and went back in where Henry slept, and he heaved the trunk to his shoulder. The cards fluttered off the top of the trunk to the rising lake and drifted away on the water's surface. The water shook like a dog, whimpered and rose one more time.

The island rocked violently, the stone overhead in the tower scraped and gnashed at each other. Rock splinters flew from its thinly circled walls. Water splashed in through the windows, and still Henry slept and still Notso stood and watched him. Water rose to his massive chest, and then Notso turned and walked into the stormy water outside, the sky black overhead, and vanished into the foam until he walked out on the eastern shore of Leelanau, clean as a whistle, thin and lean.

◆

I don't know how to say I'm a coward except to just come out and say it. I defend my year of silence now by saying truths like this you can't tell people. No one would believe it. But now I say, so the story will leave me and go on to others to determine whether they think it's true or not. For the world is full of strange things: if we turn our heads a little differently into the sleeping light, if we sit and watch the water long enough and see it change, if we look inside ourselves and wonder: had I thought one thing different, where would I be now.

◆

That's how the story got started ... that Henry's bones were out playing poker with the last wild card in his hand, in a stone lighthouse risen out of the bay, during a sudden January thaw when the sandbar let loose between the bay and Lake Michigan and the water washed out of the bay so fast, things came up that had not been seen in a long time. It was 1974 and they found the wreck of La Salle's Griffon there, the first boat of its kind to sail in the great lakes. And as soon as they found it, the tide shifted and the water rushed back into the bay, and the Griffon was lost and Henry was lost and the lighthouse hasn't been up since.

Then there's the one about how he walked into his fishing hole, leaving only a glove stuck to the hole's frosty rim. Why? Because when a man's ready to go, there's nothing can stop him.

This is the way rumor and gossip begins. They're breathed to life in the Tavern of Dreams, words drift outside with the smoke, mingle with the heat and chattering squirrels in the trees until a man or woman walking the narrow road into the Indian reservation bumps into a line of a story hanging like moss from a limb and rips it down, attaches things to it and hangs it back up for the next person to find. The story gets changed by the swell of his hands, the husk and lilt in her voice, the harshness or sweetness in the retelling, so it isn't the same, gets a new life, becomes a tale it wasn't.

But the story is still true, I'd say, though I'm an old man now and few believe me. It still bears the mark of the real on it so's people say, "I heard it next to God," or "Tie me to the side of a hog, but I couldn't have heard that one down to town. J'you?

But when all the checks are counted, I'd say Henry was a honorable man. Does he live? I don't know. But I do know on starlit nights like this, people seem to say that they see one man out on the ice, stepping in another man's track, because together, they made one man.

# POVERTY BURNING

**W**hat's that?" I asked, watching my father carry a gallon jar from the house to the barn.

"Money," he said.

"Are we poor? We never have money for clothes or movies like town kids do."

"Make the clothes you had *last* year work."

"How, Dad?"

"That's your mother's business." But year by year the hem on my dress rose up over my knees and the holes in my socks were darned with yarn that no longer matched.

My father stashed cash just like *his* father who didn't put money in the bank either. *My grandfather* buried his earnings from the farm in gallon milk bottles in a musty corner of the barn, so when the barn burned down, the bottles with their sealed lids were dug up in the wreckage, along with the Case 450 tractor, which didn't burn either, a machine as stubborn as the rest of my line.

"Put the money in the bank, Walt," my mother scolded, but my father only shook his head.

"Alice, if gallon bottles worked for Grandpa then, they can darn well work for us now."

---

Midwinter, a red Chevy, with no hood over the engine and smoke leaking out, bumped down the dirt track past our house to the abandoned farm in the valley below. There the shadows of clouds tumbled, bolts of black cloth, furling, unfurling along a snowy plain. A listing barn leaned down to the ground, as if given a bully's shove, it fell, not all the way over, but just to one knee. Beside it, a house dipped lower before the wind, as if *God* pushed its head down, saying, *you'll* do penance for poverty. Beyond, the cliff dropped a thousand rocky feet to the Lake Michigan shore, against a blue so dense, I felt pulled in, tugged out, swept along.

I heard the ping of an engine, the slip and grind of wheels on ice. Clambering out on the porch roof, the night was filled with stars. The shadow of the moon lay blue over the hills. Out on the lake a skim of ice rose and fell, breathed as if something large had come up to see and having done so, sank, effortlessly, without a sound.

That's how their car sank: window deep in the snow. A slight clatter from the engine, a deep sigh, and a rattle in the moonlight like a baby's last furious cry, as her clenched fist slides out of her mouth, down into the blanket and deeper into sleep.

Seven people got out: a thin woman wrapped in a red scarf, four children who must have left their coats in the car, and a man with a voice like a shovel digging a grave by itself. And he must have left *his* coat in the car, too, because all he had on was a shirt and pants, and the thermometer outside my window said minus two. The reason I knew the baby was there was I heard it howl like a chained up dog, until I saw a woman bend down to the rag in her arms and give it what looked like a kiss.

"Squatters, that's all they are," my father said, hauling manure out of the lower barn. "He won't make a cent with that orchard." But it was April before I got to talk to one of

them, on a day when the lake sent clouds scudding overhead, and the wind came up and flattened everything down
it could.

"You he'p her?" A little girl in a ripped dress staggered up
through the trees of my father's cherry orchard. "T'e 'ookin'
at you f'om dat window down dere." A squall wind shrieked
up, flouncing hair cloud-white, as she fixed stark pink eyes
on me. Her hair was white, stuck together with Bazooka
gum, ketchup, glue and other things I didn't even know what
they were. The sleeve of a muddy blouse trailed along the
ground from under one arm, like a dog's long pink tongue
dragged over dirt.

A whistle of wind rustled up. Below, a loose shutter banged
distantly.

"What's your name?" I scuffed over, stooped down, laid my
hoe along the ground, brushed dust from my palms to the
ground between my knees.

"Katie-e-e-e-e." A dirty thumb popped out of her mouth.
"Katie Carl. You'se?"

"Catherine Simon."

"You'se skinny an' gotsa face 'ike a skirre', but I 'ikes you
b'ack hair. How 'ong is it? My mudder has b'ack hair. How o'd
are you?"

"Going on sixteen." Although I wasn't. "You?"

"I'se not goin' on any'ting," and she leans over and looks
inside a bandage on her knee. Her once-white dress was
stained with food, dirt markings where her knees leaned
into it. Stooping down, binding her arms around her knees,
she rocked back and forth, back-and-forth, toes tipping up,
heels rocking back in the dirt. If she had a crib to bang her
head against, it seemed like she would. I wanted to hug her,
but I didn't even know her.

"Your pa dunint 'ike us. How *come* he dunint 'ike us?" She
scuffed her ragged tennis shoe in the dirt.

Since brutal honesty was my policy at fifteen, I went with that, and if she *dunint* like it, she *dunint 'ike it.*

"He says your father's not spraying your trees." Turning two pebbles over, I squatted down and banged one into hard ground. "He says the curculio worm is working its way into our trees from yours. He says if your pa doesn't spray soon, *we're* going to have to spray *your* trees to stop the bugs from coming into *ours.* And it will cost my pa money.*"*

"My pa dunint 'ike t'ees."

"No? What does he like?"

"Essee ... "A small dirty finger wriggled up her nose. "His bitch Butchie birted him six coon hounds. And once dere was dis gir' in town he kisted. He 'ikes dose t'ings, I 'magini-nin'." She set her hands on her knees, wobbling as she tried to keep her balance. A finger slipped into her left nostril. "I din't te' my mama 'bout her. You t'ink dat p'ob'y right, Cat'rin?"

"I think that's probably right."

"You 'ikes your papa?"

"No, he's too cheap. He won't even let my mother buy me *anything.* Ever. You?"

"Mine is mean 'ike our o'd dog, Shack," and pulling her finger from her nose, flicking the dried snot into the wind, she lifted her shirt showing bruises on her tummy and, swinging around, stalked downhill on little stick legs. Where our property ended and her father's began, a pale wisp of an arm motioned furiously.

*The man doesn't know how to farm,* my father said last night. *He lets his trees rot just like he lets his kids rot. You can't have the Carl girl for a friend.*

*Then what friends will I have, Dad?*

*That's up to you.*

But if the Carls were the only family around for miles, *could* it be up to me? School and town two hours away and no one willing to drive me there ... could it? And what was there to *say* to doctors' daughters and restaurant girls: Hello? I really *am* like you? Do you have black dirt for fingernail polish? Can we talk cherry trees and insects?

Glancing up over the heads of the trees to my father's red barn, then over to the house, I laid my hoe flat in the dirt so my father could not see it from a distance.

And followed Katie home.

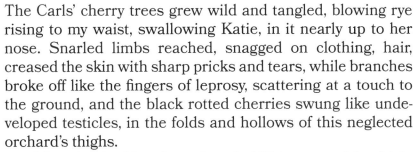

The Carls' cherry trees grew wild and tangled, blowing rye rising to my waist, swallowing Katie, in it nearly up to her nose. Snarled limbs reached, snagged on clothing, hair, creased the skin with sharp pricks and tears, while branches broke off like the fingers of leprosy, scattering at a touch to the ground, and the black rotted cherries swung like undeveloped testicles, in the folds and hollows of this neglected orchard's thighs.

I felt a shock of freedom, the wind lifting everything high. As if I could just *ignore* my duties, not *do* them and *have* no repercussions. Some day, I won't *muck* manure out of the barn, or *rake* forty acres of hay in a single afternoon.

What would my father say to me then.

"Okay!" I shouted, loping to catch up.

"Okay," she laced tiny fingers through mine. "You be *aw-wight* wit me."

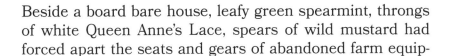

Beside a board bare house, leafy green spearmint, throngs of white Queen Anne's Lace, spears of wild mustard had forced apart the seats and gears of abandoned farm equipment, disabling rusted wheels from hay rakes, brakes off tractors, the iron molding of a flatbed trailer torn away in a great cruel arc with the thrust of strong wild corn. My father never let rust creep into a machine, unless he hadn't used it since my grandfather was running the farm. Even then, I think he oiled the sprockets on the flatbed trailer and still wiped the grime from his 1957 flatbed truck that hadn't been run since 1969.

A bell rang distantly, my mother calling and calling my father and me up from the field for a meal.

"I'll come help you tomorrow with whatever needs helping, okay?"

Katie stood, arms crossed, and snatching the dirty blouse from the ground where she'd dropped it, stopped, turned, and snapped that muddy shirt in the hard whistling air.

"I t'ot you *he'p*. You *not* he'p. You *no* good *a'tall!*" And she turned and stalked downhill, to the house, which seemed to twist and groan in the wind. A shutter banged distantly. A long field of goldenrod waved side to side over her head, until the wind leaned down and swept it flat to the cliff, exposing in the middle of a vast yellow field, a tiny figure stalking knock-kneed towards home.

Up on the hill, my mother's bell rang four times, five. I turned, turned back. Seven times, eight, I took a step toward my house, and looked back. Katie hadn't turned back to even see if I was following.

Ten.

And I swung around and trotted downhill.

"Okay!" I shouted, loping to catch up.

"T's okay," she shouted back. "You be *awight* wif me."

We toed the dirt two-track that circled the two-story clapboard house of no paint. A dirty child's face parted a torn curtain, but when I blinked, there was only the shiver of drape and then it swung still.

I felt like I was being followed. But when I glanced behind, there was only the wind sweeping the long grass flat, and above, my father's orchard rising sharply to the road.

The truth was I was going where I'd never been allowed. And I felt almost free.

Behind the house, a narrow shed door scraped open onto the plain dirt floor of the listing barn. Thin light from an overhead bulb offered no more wattage than a dirty window pierced with effort by the morning sun. Drifting out from within whisked an odor of damp clay, an uneven whirring. Slowing with a bump-bump, increasing with a clack-clack, bump-bump and bump-bump, then clack-clack, the sound gained uneven speed in tone and whistle, until a sudden *sizzle* and *pop* soared out, followed by brown drifting smoke. We coughed, wheezed, covered our faces, and poked our heads in.

Astride a low stool, bony knees to either side of a potter's wheel, sat a skeleton.

A tall woman, Mrs. Carl was nearly six feet. Fingers quieting a clay pot, spinning on the wheel. She slowed its spin as one soothes a nervous colt's throat. The turning bat creaked, groaned, whined and stopped.

And I saw that she was not dead at all.

Her hands fell into her lap. A sigh escaped her lips.

Her fingers were very long, the backs of her hands bone-thin. Her nose stood out in sharp relief to her face; the skin pulled back gaunt to her receding hair: long, curled black, held back by a single strand of potting wire ordinarily used to scrape clay from the wheel. Her hips were bone thin, under her apron, her arms the elbows of a tree sticking out from a thin trunk, with no foliage, but for the rich fall of dark hair, suggesting an elegance to her, the remains of luxury.

Beneath her potter's apron, Katie's mother was completely naked.

---

I stepped back awed. We don't go naked in our house; we don't unclothe hardly one thing. We're rural Methodists, and we're not decent unless we're covered to our chins. We don't even wear shorts, not that I'd agree. I'd strip naked in a second. Given half the solitude that Mrs. Carl had, I'd dance nude amidst these pots, seek out the fissures in the bare plank walls, the wind's mad breath a satisfaction of freedom. If *I* were her, I wouldn't get dressed either. *Imagine* what it would be like to be free of your clothes! Respectability thrown like an old coat over a porch chair. Yes, she'd thrown it all off, until freedom hung from her, a rattling cup, loose skin and bone, a clock ticking against a time when intrusion would come: a minister, a neighbor, a daughter, *insisting she-must*-get-*dressed!*

She did not once glance in our direction. And among the shadows of the barn, I felt I was not quite here either. I looked at this mother whose eyes had been on me all the while, large and dark and inquiring. I glanced 'round, so I didn't have to look into those eyes. What they held, I didn't want to know: the dank smell of secrets, pent up desires, giftedness gone crumbling with hard luck and emotion.

There's always more to a person than we know, my mother's said: what misery other people live in, what fills the rooms of their minds. *Mind your own business, make your own decisions. See what the gossips don't.*

◆

"You he'p her?" On the other side of her mother, Katie stamped her little foot. "S'e he'p dwess you, Mama." Leaning a cloud-covered head on her mother's shoulder, she whispered softly against the rich dark hair. Slinging one arm across her mother's bare back, her white burred tangles mingled with the deep, deep black. But I didn't wish to startle this mother. I didn't know what insane people were capable of. Would she throw herself at me, stick her hand inside my mouth, and with a pair of dull scissors cut off my tongue? I skirted her a little wider than I might have, although she seemed peaceful enough, patting the clay on the wheel with her thumb.

"Mama!" Tenderly taking her mother's face, Katie rotated her mother's head to face her. "Mama! Come! Now," she swung to me, "you he'p."

I skittered, turned round, swung back.

From the water barrel, Katie snatched up black pants which had not seen many washes. From my hands, she pulled the clay-splattered blouse. Underwear, she motioned me to tug down from a lightbulb overhead, and I did as she said, because I was beholden now; because I had come.

"Take dese," she slung the clothing across my outstretched arms.

"Come, Mama!" With her daughter's urging, the potter rose, and with halting steps, dragging her feet, scuffed to the back, as if she *didn't* want to go.

"Sit 'own, Mama!" Beside a broken kiln, Katie motioned me to maneuver her mother off the stool and onto a wooden chair that sat in the corner, but it was with such unwilling lethargy, it seemed she would spring up eyes wild or harden into rock. Instead, she went limp, her only defense to do nothing, like a ladybug feigns its death in the human palm.

"Ho'd her?"

"What?"

"I only said 'ho'd her.' You doan haf to ye' at me." Katie's eyes welled up. Flight rose in my throat, but I snapped at it like a dog after a hen, and then I didn't feel it any more.

Lifting her mother's limp hands by the wrist, Katie clasped them palm-to-palm to mine. They were freezing cold. I folded my thumbs over her thumbs as if we were praying as one soul, and gazed into those eyes. But I didn't know if she had a soul. I didn't know if I did either. If so, she'd end up in heaven. Ask any Methodist; they'd tell you. Don't look for gratification in this world. Denying pleasure will lead you to the promised land.

With her mother distracted by my presence, Katie snatched the brassiere from its landing place, pushed her mother's left arm through the strap, then the right. Still, one long thin breast swung free of the cloth. Mrs. Carl regarded that breast with a whimsical air, like a mother cat regards one of two kittens gone loose on the lawn while she nurses the other.

Crouching down to the floor, Katie pushed her mother's thin foot through a pair of panties, pulling them up over her mother's thigh. "Come now!" she said, "Go on!" talking to the panties. Elastic snapped on the cleft. Her mother's teeth clacked in a hiss. Katie jumped back.

With her daughter's fumbling attempts, not all body parts went where they should, and it was a ramshackle picture the potter presented when done: frock half on, one breast hanging out, pants sliding down, underwear riding off one knee, and she, standing limp as a ragamuffin doll.

Katie made the motion of pulling hands apart.

I released my hands.

Katie's eyes glowed at her mother, her mouth parted in a smile; she clapped her hands. And I saw in that gesture a child who was pleased she had carried out her responsibility. But who gave her that responsibility at such a young age, I didn't know. And what else that responsibility truly consisted of, I didn't know that either.

"Mama," Katie said, "you dwest. Cat'win hept us." For a brief second, her mother's eyes startled, as if awakening, took on a wariness, like a caught doe regards with generous mercy the barrel of the gun that will end her days. I tightened my grip on Mrs. Carl's wrists. She was swinging her head now, hands clenching and unclenching, like something coming awake, slowly, groggily, out of a dream and into the light.

Snatching her hands from mine, she yanked the blouse overhead, brassiere from her chest. Looping bra to the ceiling, she slung the shirt flying. Panties spiraled around the clay pot, pants flipped into the water barrel, and in a frenzy, Mrs. Carl slammed the potting wheel back onto its notch, sat her bony bottom back down on the stool and, flexing her long fingers, glaring once at me, once at her daughter accusingly, circled her fingers around a pot on the bat rising five feet into the air.

It did not matter that the wheel was standing perfectly still. Buck naked, she is as she was.

"Cat'win!" Katie's mouth drooped. She gave out a tearful sigh. "T'e never tay dwest. I torry," and she sunk to the floor, picking at bits of clay, dust and straw.

On the stool, Mrs. Carl turned her head and surveyed us. Through the dry dust of her tonsils, a slight wind jangled up. From her tongue, the sound of a hot night banged the shutters of windows open. Then, as if she had neglected how to form real words, as if her throat had forgotten and her tongue lay abandoned on a parched and distant road, the words rose: muted, quiet, yet wholly formed:

"I'm making a pot for my ashes. *Leave-me-be.*"

"Doan ta'k dum, Mama!"

Outside, the lake wind threw boards and twigs, small pebbles against the siding. Branches in the orchard screamed and scraped in the wind.

I shrieked out the dark door running, yanked up my hoe and chopped weeds from forty-two trees without looking back. When my mother rang the bell for supper, I turned, exhausted and glanced back down the hill. At that precise moment, Mrs. Carl emerged from the shed: bony, gaunt, naked, hair flying, standing upright in a wind so fierce it bent my father's young trees to the ground, and sent a shutter from the Carl house spiraling board over end down the cliff.

An arm came out and yanked her back in.

I didn't know whose arm. But I knew who it was tethered to. It was tethered to her.

I flew from her misery, for it was larger than I could imagine, not just in its shape, but in the dimensions of the spirit as well. I was unqualified to be breathing the same miserable air. Mrs. Carl's misery tucked its head in under her roof, pulled its elbows inside her walls and unwillingly slimmed its magnificent elephantine size to fit her skeletal body. Every breath she took spun a clay pot of sorrow.

I sat a long time with my mother, telling her about Mrs. Carl. My mother looked at me a long, long time, put down her dish rag where she had been washing dishes at the sink, picked up a shovel leaning against the screen porch and proceeded to the barn, where she dug up one of those gallon bottles with the thousand dollar bills in it, and without asking my father, stalked downhill and into the Carl barn and over to Mrs. Carl. Pulling the bills from it, she set them on the potting wheel. Then, turning to Mrs. Carl, she said: "You put these in the drawer where you keep your women's intimate things. Understand me? And when you feel right about it, you take this money out and you use it. Understand? You make a better life for yourself and your little girl."

Mrs. Carl said nothing, but her head began to nod. First a little, then a lot. Rising slowly, she wrapped her long bony fingers around my mother's hands, and for a long, long time, she didn't let go, then turned and walked over to an old cupboard in the back of the barn and taking out a knife, cutting a length from a ball of string she pulled from a musty shelf, she wrapped the string around the green bills, and put the money on the slowly turning bat. Turning to my mother, she reached forward and grasped her with a hug so hard I thought she was going to break my tiny mother, and then, nodding with great grace, she stopped, and stepped back, as if the space between them was already full of something new, lifting from a place where goodness comes like a blessing rising.

At 4 a.m. we heard the siren, as the fire engine turned and roared down the dirt road. Standing on our front porch, we watched as, in great leaping tongues of fire, the Carls' barn flamed into red. The shed burned. Flames leapt, spit, rose in black smoke, poured out the barn's vast doors, through the cracks in the foundation, the windows long broken, and it was not the smell of hay burning, or tractor diesel, or dried corn or cow manure.

It was the smell of poverty burning.

For Mrs. Carl had left the money on the potting wheel and, in the night, lit the potting wheel on fire. And now we drove down to see as the old barn fell, and when the wall fell, how that wheel spun and spun, without a hand to it or a foot to its pedal. And it was only in the musty darkness, in the shed attached to the barn, that Mrs. Carl had left the money on the potting wheel, covered it with hay and lit it on fire, for the flakes of burning bills were floating all around us, in the heated rising air.

For a long time after, I saw her in my mind, setting the barn on fire, then taking Katie and climbing the dirt track to the main road, where I think they might have stuck out their thumbs and hitched a ride south, though we never really knew for sure. For days and weeks afterward, I looked for Katie in school or on the school bus or on the road or in the few charred remains of the shed, hiding somewhere, but no, it was only my father, picking up traces of money he didn't even know were his.

# QUEEN

# OF THE CIVILIZED

# WORLD

This morning my father drove the Case tractor, raking the cut hay into rows in the south forty. My mother steered the baler, a rectangular tunnel on wheels, while my brother and our hired man stabbed ice hooks into bales she left behind, and in one fell swoop swung those bales' weight onto the bed of the 1959 Chevy flatbed truck where, in the cab, I rose from the driver's seat to reach the starter on the floor. In the southwest corner, in sunshine that turned the meadow yellow, two Gurnsey cows stood ankle deep in the pond.

Three stories in the air now, under the creak of rafters, in the 150-year-old barn that was once our grandmother's and is now our parents,' while a young screech owl sleeps on a high beam near us, my brother and I heft, with effort, one bale of hay to rest sideways on top of two others, creating a tunnel below with room for just one of us to wriggle into. I am quick into it, crawling down to lie beneath.

Over my head now, my brother jumps on the bale above me, complaining mightily that most if not *all* of the labor to build this hay castle was his (pound, pound) and therefore *he* deserves to crawl in first (pound, pound). Mr. Irritable, Mr. King of all Russia, hay tunneling takes two.

And so, when I am done considering where I will place a TV in the three inches of space I allot for it, and where the big armchair in the four inches of my left-hand corner, and where my right toe is poked might go my .45 rpm record player I got for my tenth birthday, then and *only* then, shall I decide whether I'll crawl out and let my brother come in, or whether I might just take my afternoon nap.

And while I am under the hay listening to his ongoing harangue, a monologue no less in words than any presidential address, it is rest that takes over, sleep sifting into weary muscles, until, in the dusky shadows of late afternoon, I close my eyes and dream. I am a soldier-girl in a war against cowardice, Joan of Arc, Queen of the Civilized World. I fight the ignorant, the uninformed, treacherous fools who slaughter innocents. My horse, clad in mail responds to my shifting weight, stepping, turning sideways, swinging around at the touch of my knee, as we challenge those who threaten the future of our young.

It is dusk when I wake. The dinner bell clangs and clangs for the family and farmhands to wash up at the outside tap. I take my time: flicking off my imaginary TV in the corner, turning the knob on the record player so the disk — that isn't there — slows and stops. I back out from under my hay bale, yawning and stretching with the soundest of sleeps, and sink back onto my heels. Across from me, on a high barn beam, in the dusk, the yellow headlights of a screech owl's eyes ponder me. As if in some complicity, he winks once, and lifting his massive wings flies up, up through the dusk near the rafters, then turning, swoops out through the barn doors flung wide, nearly brushing the head of my brother who, standing in the doorway, hands on hips, brushes off its wing beat with a furious arm's arc, his foot impatiently tap-tapping, tap-tapping: Mr. Irritability, Mr. Miffed, Mr. King of All Russia.

"Aren't you coming?! She's called you *three* times!"

And though my body will brush past the enemy and walk across the road to home for dinner, my horse and I, and our trusty owl, have just broken through the front lines.

# ABOUT THE AUTHOR

Carolyn J. Lewis received her Bachelor of Arts from New York University's Gallatin Division, and her law degree from Jacob D. Fuchsberg Law School in New York. She was a legal, scholarly, and literary editor, and an award-winning short story writer. Her stories were nominated for the Pushcart Prize by Maxine Kumin, Poet Laureate of New Hampshire, guest editor of *Kalliope*; accepted into an anthology on rural writing by Fred Chappell, Poet Laureate of North Carolina; placed in the semifinals of the Pirate's Alley William Faulkner Award; placed as a semifinalist in the Heekin Group Foundation's Tara Fellowship in Short Fiction; placed as the lead story by Geraldine Sanford, guest editor of the *South Dakota Review*; noted by the *Sycamore Review*, Purdue University, as a unique new voice, in the Novel & Short Story Market; and was invited to be read on Interlochen Public Radio for the Michigan Writers Hour. She also served as guest editor for Northwest Michigan's literary journal: *The Dunes Review.*

The women in her family have been beekeepers since 1861, supplying the Old Mission Peninsula, Michigan, cherry farmers with bees to fertilize their trees. The family still farms on her great-great-great-grandmother's land, but the bees are leaving and no one knows why. A daughter of the land, her fondest activity was talking to the 600 year old trees, asking where all the bees had gone.

Made in the USA
Columbia, SC
01 September 2019